$10 MILLION INSTAGRAM FUNNEL

THE **BLUEPRINT** FOR ONLINE COACHES

BRIAN MARK

ISBN 978-1-0694456-0-5 Paperback
ISBN 978-1-0694456-1-2 Hardcover

Book design by Autumn Skye.

Printed in the United States of America.

First printing edition 2025.

Outwork Publishing
British Columbia, Canada

CONTENTS

FOREWORD

FROM LAYNE NORTON:

I am a scientist and a lifter by trade. I don't have a background in marketing or sales. When I got into the fitness industry 20+ years ago, it seemed like it would be impossible to make a good living without using seedy marketing tactics or sleezy sales strategies. The only people I saw crushing it in fitness financially were people who were using these sorts of tactics. Fear mongering, drastically exaggerated claims, false promises, and outright lies were the norm. I resigned myself to the fact that maybe I could be successful but I'd never be able to ascend to a level of great financial success. I made my peace with it because I cared more about my integrity and reputation in the industry than I did making tons of money.

That said, I like money as much as the next person and wanted to have financial success, I just didn't want to feel like I was selling my soul to do it. Over time, I was able to see some financial success and build my business slowly. Along with this success came offers from various marketers and sales people with 'opportunities' to 10x my business or increase my sales by some insane amount. I interviewed many of these marketing/sales companies and people over the course of the last decade but only ever hired a couple for short periods of time. My experience in these interviews was that most of those companies wanted me to fundamentally change how I promoted my products & services. They wanted me to use fear or exaggerated claims to sell my products and services. It was very clear they didn't have a good idea of who I was or my brand and reputation. Of the companies and people I did hire, I never saw returns on my investment and there were ALWAYS excuses. We weren't spending enough money on marketing, or we were spending too much money. They would also say I needed to make more unique content for the marketing which I always felt odd since I have tens of thousands of pieces of content that already exist online. Why would I pay a marketing company to make MORE work for me? So I gave up on the idea of marketing and sales companies.

Then in late 2022, Brian and Cole invited me to speak at their event. Brian was someone I had mentored as a nutrition coach in the past and had met at a camp I held in Canada in 2017. At the time, I didn't really want to do another speaking engagement but Brian wouldn't take no for an answer. I was concerned however because I saw their business was around helping coaches make more sales. I had seen some of the events of other companies who made promises about increasing coaching sales. In my experience it was a lot of chest thumping and hype but almost no actionable information or tangiable ways to improve sales, but since I knew Brian I decided to agree to speak. I figured that even if the rest of the talks were garbage, at least mine would be good.

As I watched Brian and Cole talk about what to do, I realized their sales advice was very similar to how I give nutrition advice. There was no magic secret to 10x your business. It was about consistency with content, the type of content, and engaging with your audience consistently. Not only that, but Brian and Cole were emphatic about the basic steps needed to increase sales. They weren't hiding it behind the veil of secrecy. They were putting it out there as a basic process anyone could do and they also held their coaches accountable with little patience for excuses. I also got a chance to speak with many of their clients who absolutely raved about Brian and Cole. I was impressed.

So a few years later when I felt like I could do better with my own coaching sales, I hired Brian and Cole to help coach our company. What I found was that they were very systematic in how they approached things with copy, generating leads, converting leads, and trying to determine where they failure points in the process were so that they could determine what steps needed to be taken in order to improve the process. I hired them for 90 days in which time they said I should see a 30% increase in sales by the end and that is exactly what they delivered. They also never tried to get me to change my voice and were very respectful on occasion when I said I felt like some marketing verbiage was pushing me to feel uncomfortable. They were emphatic that it had to be in alignment with who I am, not just what generates attention.

What I admire about Brian and Cole is that they are very straightforward and direct with what they know works and the steps that need to be taken to achieve it. There is NO fluff or BS. It's not magic. It's not a secret. But it works. If you follow the steps and do the work, the process works, which is why I recommend Brian's book and material if you want to figure out how to improve coaching sales.

START HERE

Scan this QR code to create your account and unlock all the resources included in this book.

CHAPTER 1

$500 TO MY NAME IN BALI

I woke up at 6 AM in the morning in a foreign country. I barely remember getting to Bali. I was drenched in sweat, in a tiny bed, in a small room, in an Airbnb.

*Sh*t, I'm hungover.*

I got out of bed and walked outside to see the streets of Bali. It was the first time traveling outside of Canada, and I'd chosen a third world country.

How I got here? Funny story. Let me condense the long story.

I'm from Calgary, Alberta. I met a girl. We fell in love. And we planned to move to Australia. A month before my flight, it felt like the wrong move. So, I cancelled. She went to Australia without me. We did long distance for five months and it failed. She broke up with me over a video call.

I booked a one-way trip to Australia, and hoped I'd change her mind. When I arrived, she never answered my call.

I was faced with a decision. I could fly back to Canada—empty handed—or I could figure out a way to enjoy my time since I had already traveled to Australia. I had never been on a plane before. So, that was a big trip for me.

I decided that I was going to live my life. I jumped out of a plane for the first time. I got my first tattoo in Australia. I even got wasted with a friend I met, and we went out to a casino and gambled three thousand dollars.

That night I gambled three thousand dollars, however, I *may* have gone overboard.

Wasted, forgetting about the fact that I was on the other side of the world, I dwindled my bank account down to five hundred dollars.

The next morning, I took a flight to Denpasar, Bali. Since I was traveling on that side of the world, I thought I might as well explore.

So, that's how I got to Bali. Hungover. With five hundred dollars in my bank account.

I left the Airbnb and I tried to get my bearings.

What... is... this?

The sidewalk had holes everywhere. I watched a three-legged dog cross the road. Half of its fur was gone. I walked for two miles and couldn't believe my eyes. Scooters raced by at Mach 9 speed. Cars weaved in and out of traffic. Everyone honked their car horns like madmen.

What is this place?

I walked by a local market and watched a live chicken get his head chopped off— that was the final straw for me. I went back to the Airbnb.

I didn't know anyone in Bali, and I hadn't realized yet that I didn't have any money. I was still hungover from the casino night.

At the Airbnb, I was greeted by the host. I asked how I could get around, and they told me they could rent me a scooter for 100,000.

I went to an ATM to get money. Thankfully, I found out that 100,000 rupiah was the equivalent of ten Canadian dollars. I put my card into the ATM and instantly felt a wave of anxiety fall over my entire body. My balance read $515.

The night before came racing back.

"One thousand on black."

"One thousand on red."

"One thousand on black."

Three thousand dollars—gone.

*F**k!*

I took out two hundred CAD and went back to my Airbnb. After renting my scooter, I started ripping around the streets of Bali, trying to find my way. Little did I know that this trip was going to change my entire life.

ADVERSITY INTO OPPORTUNITY

I had no idea how I was going to get home. I had five hundred dollars to last me three weeks. Thankfully, I bought my return ticket home before my drunken fiasco at the casino. Bali was also cheap to live in; my Airbnb was twenty dollars a night and food was about twenty dollars a day. Despite Bali being cheap to live, I had enough money for one to two weeks max. I'd spent six months saving money to go on a trip at some point, and I had managed to blow that savings on three Roulette table bets.

In Canada, I'd *tried* to start an online fitness business, but I never took it seriously. I posted on social media, but I was inconsistent. I had a few clients, but I wasn't serious about my business. I had made some money, but it was nothing to write home about.

I knew if I didn't find a way to make money while in Bali, I was going to be in a rough spot. It felt like if I didn't make money on that trip, I was going to die. The largest amount I had ever collected from an online coaching package was two hundred dollars for a twelve-week meal plan. I assumed that people would only pay me for the time I spent organizing their plan. It took me about six hours to do twelve hours' worth of meals. So, I charged thirty dollars per hour and thought that was a high amount.

In Bali, I needed to make about five thousand dollars, and I wasn't going to make that off twelve-week meal plans. I had to think outside of the box.

At the time, my confidence level in my ability to sell was almost zero. I wasn't born an entrepreneur; I was forced into it by necessity. At fourteen, I sold newspaper subscriptions door-to-door, and I won *The best in Calgary*. At nineteen years old, I sold cell phones at TELUS and made a commission on my sales. At age twenty, I worked for a life coaching company. So, I knew how to sell, I just didn't have the confidence to sell my online coaching program. Looking back, I realize it was because I didn't believe in myself enough to believe I could pull it off.

In Bali, however, I didn't have a choice.

I really felt like if I didn't figure out how to make money online that I would die in Bali. That sounds like an exaggeration, I'm sure, but on some level, I believed I wouldn't make it home unless I figured it out.

So, I did.

Working at a local coffee shop one day, I came up with the idea for "Soft to Shredded." I put together a graphic and I called a local supplement company in Calgary. They knew me and said they would put together a prize package for a challenge if I wrote their supplements into the meal plans I created.

They gave me a $250 prize package to give away. That gave me leverage when I published content. I made a graphic using Canva and called the program the "Soft to Shredded 6-Week Challenge."

I partnered with DYNAMIS Nutrition on the program, and new clients received a promo code to use on their products. DYNAMIS also gave me a prize package.

I spent a full day planning out the six-week challenge. Then I posted on Facebook and Instagram. That was the start to a new beginning.

"Start before you're ready," was the first entrepreneurship lesson I learned.

I announced that I would take on ten clients who wanted to lose body fat, gain lean muscle, and get into the best shape of their lives. Most of my network came from when I worked as a bartender in Calgary, Alberta. A bunch of people I knew from nightclubs, so when I started posting about my new offer; my current network was the first to express interest.

I decided that I would find a way to get ten people into the "Soft to Shredded" Challenge and that's exactly what I did. Every morning I woke up at five in the morning. Five a.m. in Bali was two in the afternoon back in Canada. I spent my workdays messaging people on Facebook and asking if they were interested in joining the Soft to Shredded 6-Week Challenge. It was a shot in the dark. I had no idea what I was doing, but thankfully through the relationships I established during my time as a nightclub bartender and manager, I was able to gather some interest.

Once I had someone's attention and they were interested, I set up a phone call. All I needed was a Wi-Fi connection, and I could Facebook audio call them through messenger for free.

I spent seven days building relationships in my DMs, scheduling Facebook audio messenger calls, and recruiting people into my Soft to Shredded program.

I didn't have a Stripe or payment processor system set up, so I had participants send me $499 e-transfers. In one week, I collected five thousand dollars.

I did that all while being on the other side of the world, in a third world country, with nothing but a Wi-Fi connection and Facebook audio calls. That's when I realized, if I could make five thousand dollars in Bali, I sure as hell could do the same thing back in Canada with access to more resources.

I spent the rest of my time in Bali working on my business and serving my six-week challenge participants. When I got back to Canada, I put in my two-week's notice at work. April 2016 is the last time I had a full-time, nine to five job.

From then on, I made a commitment. I was going to make $10,000 a month as an online fitness coach.

As of this moment, I just hit my third, million-dollar month in a row. Two weeks prior, I was meditating and I had the thought, *I need to write a book.* The idea came to me like a sudden intuition. More specifically, I knew I needed to document the exact process I used to not only start my business, but to also generate more than $30,000,000 in sales during the past six years.

I started out just like you.

I was raised in a lower income family. Call me the trailer park boy. My family worked hard but they worked hard at jobs they didn't love. I watched my uncle work ten- to twelve-hour shifts at his security job to put food on the table for our family for more than five years.

I always knew I wanted to do something big with my life, I just didn't know what that was going to look like. I had dreams of being a pro athlete. When I became a pro fitness model, I realized there was zero money involved. That was incredibly disappointing because I spent two years chasing the idea of becoming a pro, only to realize that there was no monetization other than free supplements that came from sponsors I had to reach out to. After becoming a pro, I quickly realized I needed to start my own business.

The problem was, I had no idea how to start a business.

I knew someone who was an online fitness coach. She lived in the same city as me, Tea Cuk, and she did an incredible job running her business. She had one hundred clients who all paid her $250 per month.

If I could make $25,000 per month, man, what a life I would have, I thought.

I asked her to get coffee, so I could pick her brain. She gave me some pointers, but I ultimately had to rely on myself. I spent the next few months waddling around trying to figure out how to start my business while working as a full-time bartender.

Then the Bali trip happened, and everything changed. That trip put me into a "do or die" situation. I had to figure it out, or I would be screwed.

I wrote this book because it's the information I wish I had when I first got started. I wish I had a comprehensive, start to finish guide that told me exactly what to do to turn my Instagram into a money-making machine. It would have saved me from hiring the wrong mentors, wasting hundreds of thousands of dollars on ads, associating myself with the wrong people, and years of trial and error.

In this book, I'm going to give you the blueprint to take whatever your passion is and use Instagram to go viral, get more customers, attract your ideal clients, book sales calls with interested prospects, and convert them into your high-ticket offer.

By the end of this book, you will have the exact advice I would give myself if I wanted to start a new Instagram account with the goal of turning my passion into a million dollar business.

This book doesn't contain any fluff. My goal is to give you tangible, real, actionable advice that you can use immediately to improve your profile, your content, your messaging, your sales call and ultimately make you more money.

I hope you're just as excited as I am.

Let's dive in!

CHAPTER 2

THE INSTAGRAM FUNNEL BLUEPRINT

In this chapter, I am going to break down the exact blueprint I use to generate more than $1,000,000 in cash-collected sales every month. It's crazy to even consider that's my income right now. I checked my Stripe account at five in the afternoon on a Friday and it's showing I collected $38,600 today. The majority of my income is generated through Instagram. And when I say the majority, I mean about 80% of revenue. I believe Instagram is the single best platform you can build a business on in 2025. I don't think there is a better vehicle to grow your business. Sure, there's Facebook. But it has messaging restrictions. As soon as you send out too many messages, Facebook will block your account from sending new messages. That makes it nearly impossible to get any work done.

There's also TikTok, but its messaging feature is the worst. Plus, people don't use TikTok for messaging; they use it to watch short form videos.

YouTube doesn't allow you to have a one-on-one conversation with someone in your comment section. It's great for nurturing leads and prospects, but YouTube isn't so great at converting leads.

And who could forget podcasting? I have a podcast, and I've published more than one thousand episodes. The podcast was an absolute gamechanger for my business, however, it was not responsible for directly impacting my revenue in terms of converting clients. That happened, and continues to happen, through Instagram.

Since this is my book, I'm not going to bore you with Instagram statistics or features. I'm going to give you how I've used Instagram to generate $30,000,000 in sales. With my framework, you'll have a fundamental understanding of what you need to do on Instagram to go viral, grow your business, and make money.

That being said, you have to have a baseline understanding of Instagram and understand the purpose of the platform. If you understand Instagram, it will help you align yourself with Instagram's purpose so you can ultimately achieve your goals.

WHEN WE HELP INSTAGRAM ACHIEVE ITS GOALS, WE ACHIEVE OUR GOALS.

Instagram is a business. The goal of its business is to make money. So how does Instagram make its money? It sells your attention to advertisers. And your attention is worth a lot of money.

Meta, the parent company of Instagram, generated $113 billion in ad revenue in 2023. *Damn*! Attention is the new currency.

Instagram needs *you* in order to make money. The platform can't sell your attention to advertisers unless they *have* your attention. Instagram makes money by selling your attention to advertisers. They have your attention when you consume content. When Instagram has your attention, it shows you content that you're likely to consume. That is how the algorithm works, which is why your newsfeed is currently full of content that is similar to content you've consumed before.

CHAPTER 2

Instagram's goal is to keep you on the platform longer because if they keep you on the platform, that means they can sell more of your attention to advertisers.

So how would does Instagram keep you on the platform longer? They show you content you're most likely to consume based on your previous consumption behavior.

Why is this relevant to you, and why should you care? Because if you want to win the game of virality on Instagram, you need to understand the rules. The rules of the game are very simple: When you create content that captures people's attention, they will share it, like and comment on your post, watch it again, tag a friend, potentially hate on you in the comments, or send you DMs about your post. If this happens, you're creating content that aligns with Instagram's goals. You're keeping people on the platform longer. As a result of you keeping people on Instagram longer, the platform pushes your content to an even wider audience.

But wait, it gets better. Not only will Instagram push your content out to a wider audience, it will push your content out to a wider audience that is like the audience that has already interacted with your content.

It's never been easier to grow a business on social media then it is in 2025. The goal is simple: Create content that is engaging and keeps people on Instagram longer. When you do this, you help Instagram with its goals. That helps the platform keep more people's attention, which it can then sell to advertisers.

Because you are help Instagram with it goals, they will help you with your goals. As a result of creating engaging content, Instagram will push your content out to a wider audience, which leads to more people following you and engaging with your content, which will push your content further and further into the newsfeed. Before you know it, you're an Instagram gangster.

Alright, that's fun. How *exactly* does it work?

Let's break it down.

This is the Instagram Marketing funnel.

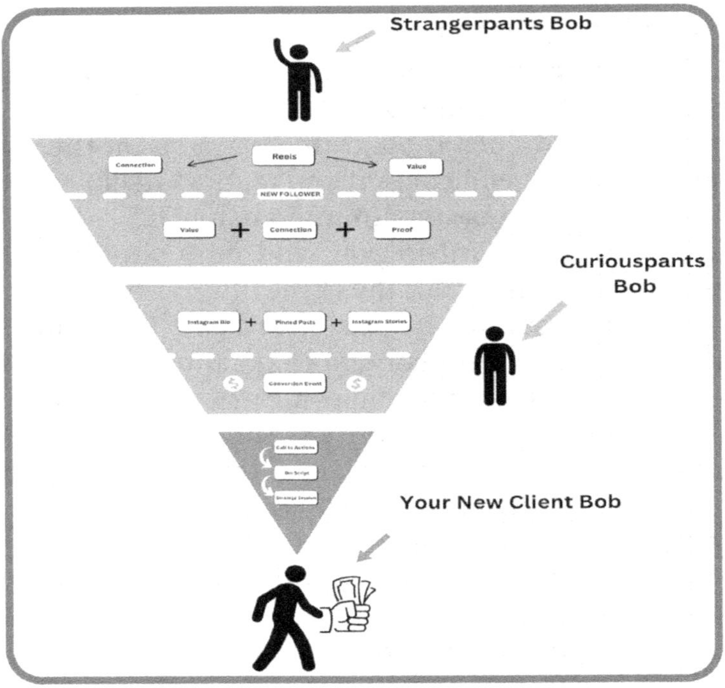

If you've done any research into internet marketing, or you don't live under a rock, you've heard about funnels. The traditional funnel is simple. You create an ad that is shown to a wide audience. That ad sends the audience to a landing page. The landing page is optimized to collect data from your prospective clients. Once you have data from your prospective clients, you push them through your conversion vehicle. Your conversion vehicle can be a sales call, a webinar, a free training, etc. Whatever it is, your goal is to be seen by a wide audience, have people end up on your landing page, collect their data, then close the deal.

Here's the thing. Your Instagram account *is* a marketing funnel. Let me explain.

Instagram Reels are the top of the funnel. The purpose of Instagram Reels is to get pushed out to a wider audience. Most people post below-average Instagram Reels for less than thirty days. They get five hundred views on every video. And they get butt-hurt that they're not growing on social media, so they quit.

Well, let me put you onto some game.

Not only do you *need* to create Instagram Reels, but you also *need* to create Instagram Reels that align with Instagram's goals. So, your Instagram Reels need to spark an emotion. These emotions can be:

- Curiosity
- Humor
- Anger
- Love
- Compassion
- Sadness

It doesn't matter which emotion you choose, but your Instagram Reel needs to capture people's attention to the point that they *have to* watch your video. They have to consume your content. They have to share, like and comment on your post.

That's the whole purpose of Instagram Reels. Personally, I've grown my Instagram account off of Instagram Reels. When I say my entire account, I mean 95% of content I post on Instagram are Reels.

I'm a huge fan of Reels—not only for the fact that they've proven to get me in front of a wider audience, but also because of the fact that when I'm repeatedly talking on camera, I'm activating the parasocial relationship. This refers to the relationship that an audience member has with a member of the media, or someone they watch on TV. The same neurons fire inside of someone's mind when they're watching someone on video that fire in their brain if they're having a conversation with a friend. That means the more you talk on video, the more you develop a deeper relationship with members of your audience.

There are two types of Instagram Reels you should post to be seen by a wider audience. They are **Connection** Reels and **Value** Reels.

The reason most people fail at Instagram is because they post only one style of content, and it's typically value content. When it doesn't work (because their content sucks), they give up.

You can't *just* post Value Reels. If you only post value Reels, you become a preacher on social media, and no one likes listening to someone who's constantly preaching. That's the fastest way to get an unfollow. I'm sure that's not how you want to be perceived.

The biggest thing I need you to understand before we go further is that people **aren't purchasing your product**. People **are purchasing you**.

If you're an online coach, people don't buy your program, they're buying *you* as their coach. That's why it's imperative that you show your audience who you are. You can't only show the polished, done up, dressed up, best version of yourself.

You need to show the *real* shit.

The *personal* stuff.

The *struggles* you've been through.

The *adversity* you've had to overcome.

The *wins* you've experienced.

You need tell your audience who you are, and they need to fall in love with you as a person. They can also hate you as a person, too. That helps you in the algorithm. And when they *do* fall in love with you as a person, it's a lot easier for you to put an offer in front them.

So be yourself.

If only it were that easy.

When I say "put yourself out there" on social media, it's more than a challenging task. Did you know that public speaking is often a person's No. 1 fear? People are more afraid to speak in public than they are of death.

Isn't that astounding?

I understand why people have a hard time putting themselves out there on social media. It's the ultimate form of public speaking. You're exposing yourself to an audience of strangers, and some of those strangers are going to be ruthless. I call the keyboard warriors "bridge trolls."

But most of you are holding yourselves back from building your dream businesses because you're afraid of what *strangerpantsbob224443* is going to say to you in your Instagram comments. Or worse, you're worried what your mom, brother, or your best friend is going to say about you.

And again. Listen, I get it. The amount of hate I experienced when I first started my business was absolutely disgusting. It's the age-old analogy of crabs in the bucket. Everyone wants you to be successful—just not more successful than them. Which is why, when you make the full-blown commitment that you're going to build your online business you have to understand that it's going to come with hate—a lot of hate. Some of the hate you'll get will come from people you least expect.

Hate will come from:

- People you've known for years
- People you used to hang out with
- Family members who have something to say about your content

You're going to have to understand that putting yourself out there is going to come with hate, and you're going to have to welcome it. Posting on social media to build your business is the ultimate form of personal development. There is nothing you can do on this planet outside of posting on social media that will develop you into someone who is absolutely bulletproof and unphased. Social media isn't for the faint of heart.

The percentage of people who are *actually* willing to walk through the door that is social media? It's 1%. For real. The percentage of people who are *actually* willing to do the work involved in posting on social media every day, seven days a week, 365 days of the year—1%.

That's why it's easy to be successful! That's why you're reading this book. You *want* to be the 1%! You want to be the anomaly—the one who stands out from the crowd and goes against the grain. You *want* to be the one who decides that there's not a force on Earth that will stand between you and your goals. You are the 1%.

I'm telling you, it's all on the other side of posting on social media. But you can't just post content for the sake of posting. You're here because you want to build a business. So, the question you need to ask yourself is: Who am I posting content for?

YOU NEED AN IDEAL CLIENT

Remember what we spoke about with the Instagram algorithm? The algorithm customizes your newsfeed based on the content you consistently produce. If you spend your day watching cute, cat videos, when you log on Instagram you're going to have a lot of cute, cat videos in your newsfeed.

This is the ultimate advantage when it comes to creating content. If you start speaking specifically to your ideal client (the person you would like to work with on social media), Instagram is going to learn over some time who that ideal client is, and then start recommending your content to your ideal client.

Why?

If that ideal client finds your page and consumes content in which you're speaking directly to them, then they're likely to stay on the platform for longer.

So, you can't be a generalist when you post on social media. First off, that's boring! No one follows a generalist. Second, every person you look up to—they started as a specialist before they became famous.

Tony Robbins? He was famous for helping people getting rid of their phobias in an instant. That's how he became famous.

Gary Vaynerchuk? He was famous for his wine show, in which he posted every day on YouTube about wine tasting. He became known as the "Wine Guy."

Alex Hormozi? He was famous for Gym Launch. He built his entire brand on helping gym owners build their business by using advertising. Everyone knew Alex from Gym Launch before they knew Alex as Alex Hormozi.

Just like Tony, Gary, and Alex, you must be a specialist. Not only is this an advantage for the algorithm, but this is also an advantage for your business. If you're a generalist, like a Mindset Coach, you're instantly competing against Tony Robbins for clients because *he* is a mindset coach.

If someone is going to pay five thousand dollars for an online coaching program, why would they hire you when they could hire Tony Robbins for the exact same service?

If you niche down, however, and you're a mindset coach for fathers who are also entrepreneurs? That's a different story. You create content specifically for fathers who are in entrepreneurship and your content speaks directly to them.

When your ideal client finds your page, not only does your content speak to them, but it also speaks to their specific pains, struggles, goals, dreams, and aspirations. As a result, they feel connected to you and your page. If an entrepreneurial father is deciding who he wants to hire for mindset work, he *could* still hire Tony Robbins (let's be honest, he's a GOAT), or he could hire the guy he's been following on social media for three months and every single post resonated with him and his specific pain points and struggles.

You just made five thousand dollars because you decided to be a specialist.

Before I wrote this book for online coaching businesses, I decided that I was going to be the No. 1 Business Coach for Online Fitness Coaches. That's exactly what I did. I spent seven years pursuing that goal. While doing so, I cemented myself as the No. 1 Business Coach for Online Fitness Coaches, and we've worked with more than ten thousand trainers. At this point, we serve clients around the world.

I could have written a general business book before I started my venture to be the No. 1 business coach for online trainers. Would it have been successful? Not a chance.

While other business coaches in my space deviated and started helping CEOs or gyms, or sold their business, I stayed true to my mission. I cemented myself as the authority in the space that gave me the ability to be able to write this book for you.

You need to be a specialist, and you need to be the best damn specialist in your space. You're in a one-of-one situation. As soon as you decide your niche and who your avatar is, you need to decide who your ideal client is. It's not enough to just have that person as your avatar. You need to be the best damn coach in your industry for that specific avatar, and you need to be proud of it.

We must speak it, before we can become it.

Long before I became the No. 1 coach for online fitness coaches, I spoke it into existence.

Go and listen to my the first thirty episodes of my podcast, and you'll hear me say, even six years ago, "This is the No. 1 show for online fitness coaches."

Know Who to Speak To

The only way you became an expert in your area is to have some experience in the field you want to be a coach in. Otherwise, you shouldn't be a coach (but that's beside the point). I'm assuming you have experience in the field you want to coach in. And the experience doesn't have to mean you've worked with clients in the field; the experience really means that you've experienced what you're teaching people how to go through.

For that reason, your best, ideal client is your past self.

Think about:

- The past pains you went through
- The past problems you experienced
- The past adversities you overcame
- The past lessons you learned
- The past dreams, goals, desires, and aspirations you had

I want you to think about you when you first got started. What were:

- Your biggest pain points regarding your journey?
- Some of the frustrations you had while getting started?
- Some of the things you did on a day-to-day basis to solve your problems.
- Some of the myths you believed to be true about your industry.
- You searching for?
- You researching online.
- How did you try to find productive solutions when you were looking online?
- What products did you purchase to try and solve those problems?
- What was your social life like?
- What about your levels of confidence?
- What was your "emotional home," aka, what was the primary emotional state you were living in?
- How was that impacting your personal life?

Understanding your answers to these questions on a deep and fundamental level will give you an understanding of who your best, ideal client is. That is how you start.

Homework

I'm giving you some homework. Sit down with pen and paper or Microsoft Word and take some time to reflect on the questions above. This is going to help you clarify the avatar you should be speaking to on social media.

I recommend all online coaches get started by speaking to their old selves.

As you gain more experience in the industry, and you start posting content, you'll attract a certain type of client with your story. You'll think that you're speaking to your old self, but in reality your story is meant to help a specific type of person.

So, as you share your value, as you contribute to social media, and as you post your content, people are going to start reaching out to you.

You're going to sign your first ten clients. Then, you're going to look at the data.

Do Not Do This Next Step Until you Have Ten or More Clients

First, we speak to our old selves, which attracts a certain type of client. Once you sign your first few clients based off the information in this book and by posting your story online, then you can get more specific and home in on your ideal client. Something I've told my clients for years is: Your ideal client chooses you. So, pay attention to the data.

Artificial Intelligence (AI) is at the tip of our fingers; all you have to do is ask it the right questions.

Here's How to Get Real Specific with Your Ideal Client Once You Have Ten or More Clients

I want you to review your clients, and I want you to identify:

- How old they are
- What they do for work
- What their biggest struggle was coming in
- What their main goals are
- Why they choose you as a coach
- Their relationship status
- Their parenthood status

Identify the answers to these questions first. Then go to ChatGPT, and type in this prompt:

"Please help me create a detailed profile of my ideal customer. This is my ideal customer (insert answers to the questions above) by answering the following questions:

1. **Fears**: What are their top three fears related to their problem or the solution?
2. **Frustrations**: What daily challenges or frustrations do they face regarding this issue?
3. **Goals**: What are they trying to achieve that my product or service can help with?
4. **Motivations**: What emotions or desires drive their decision-making process (e.g., fear, comfort, status)?
5. **Myths**: What misconceptions do they have about their problem or the solutions available?

"Please summarize these insights into a table format, labeling the X-axis 1–10 (representing severity or importance), and the Y-axis with the categories: Fears, Frustrations, Goals, Motivations, and Myths they believe.

"Please include any relevant information that you believe I will be able to use in order to create high-value content for them that attracts them on a regular basis to buy my stuff."

SUMMARY

In this chapter, we discussed why you need to start going all-in on social media, the importance of letting go of your fear of judgement or criticism, and the fact that you *have* to be a specialist. I also provided you a framework to uncover who your ideal client is, regardless of if you're just getting started or you're already working with clients.

If you are a new online coach, then you need to sit down and get super clear on your own pains, problems, struggles, goals, and motivations when you first started on the journey you now want to coach people through. Doing so will give you the information you need to be able to create high value content that converts clients. Do not move onto the next chapter until you've completed the homework in this chapter.

If you are an experienced online coach, do the damn work to get your customer research done using the prompt I gave you. Doing so will give you a clearer understanding of exactly what type of messaging you need to put on social media to attract clients.

Once you have completed the action items in this chapter, you can move onto the next. Until then, get to work, and I'll see you in the next chapter.

CHAPTER 3

YOUR PROFILE IS YOUR BUSINESS CARD

Imagine you walk into a first date with someone you really like. They sit across the table from you. They're all done up and they are excited to see you. Then, you look down at your clothes, which are from the local thrift shop. You realize you forgot to shower and you may have forgotten to brush your teeth.

That's how if comes across if you post low quality content you filmed with your iPhone 3 in your basement. Here's the thing, your Instagram account is your marketing funnel. The Reels you post are pushed out to a wider audience of complete strangers and then that wider audience of strangers clicks on your profile. When they land on your profile, that wider audience of strangers is going to make the single most important decision they need to make if you want to turn your Instagram into a lead generation machine. They will decide to follow you or not.

The *only* way they're going to follow you is if they get a great first impression. When you meet a person for the first time, your brain makes a snap decision within the first three seconds regarding whether you want to interact with that person or not. That three second rule applies to you and your social media as well. When someone lands on your social media profile, within three seconds they're going to see everything they need in order to determine whether or not you build a profitable online business or you make zero money.

To follow, or not to follow

We're going to cover, step by step, the exact breakdown of how you need to optimize your Instagram profile. I'm going to teach you how I generated more than one hundred thousand leads in 2024, which allowed me to generate $10,000,000 in revenue for the year. Without further ado, let's dive in.

THE 6 STEPS TO TURNING YOUR INSTAGRAM PROFILE INTO A SALES MACHINE.

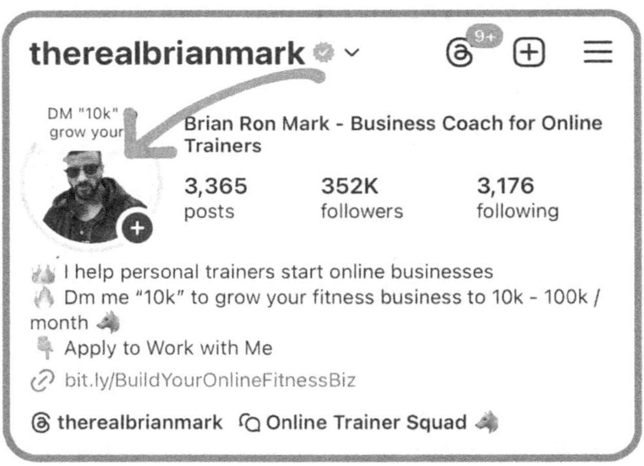

Step 1: Profile Picture

We absolutely must start this conversation with your profile picture. You only get one profile picture, and most of that three-second impression you get from others is going to be devoted to the image you choose for your profile picture. Not only is your profile picture important for your first impression, but it's also important for lead generation efforts we're going to cover farther into this book.

When you're direct messaging prospects, the only thing they can see is that tiny version of your profile picture in their DMs. I promise you, if you have a profile photo you took with your iPhone 3 in a dark room or your profile photo is of you with your two best friends—you're not going to look like an authority and it'll massively affect your income.

A profile photo is so small that we think that it doesn't matter, but that photo can be a deciding factor for whether someone replies to your message. So, let me put you on some game. Here's exactly what you need to do to get a fantastic profile picture.

First, you need to have great lighting. If you can't afford a professional photographer—that's fine. You don't even need a ring light. Instead, take your profile picture in front of a window and have the light facing you, meaning that you are looking in the direction of the light. That will give you a well-lit picture.

Second, you need to be smiling or you need to look like an authority in your space. If your profile photo shows you snowboarding, but you're trying to be an online coach, your audience will be confused.

If you're an online fitness coach, a photo showing that you're jacked is perfect. If you're a business coach, use a photo where you look like an authority on stage on a podcast. If you're a real estate agent, use a photo of you in a suit or in front of a "sold" sign. You get the point. Your profile picture needs to scream "I'm an authority in this space."

Third, you need to make sure that your face is visible in the photo. Most people post profile photos of their entire body from head to foot. But the problem with that is when you go into direct messages, your prospects can barely make out the shape of you, let alone see your face. You need to make sure that you have a clean shot. I recommend using a crop from your mid-belly or chest area to the top of your head. That will make you seem more approachable and your face will be more recognizable when you're in someone's DMs.

Fourth, I recommend removing the background of your profile photo and adding a color. You can go to PFPMaker.com and upload your profile photo. Then you can remove the background and add a color to your photo. I personally think adding a color background makes you stand out and makes your photo stand out more.

The profile picture I use is one where I look like a baddy (or so I think), and I removed the background and added a white background. I like the minimal look of that. I've also used profile pictures where I'm smiling and I have a blue background. I like the look of that, too.

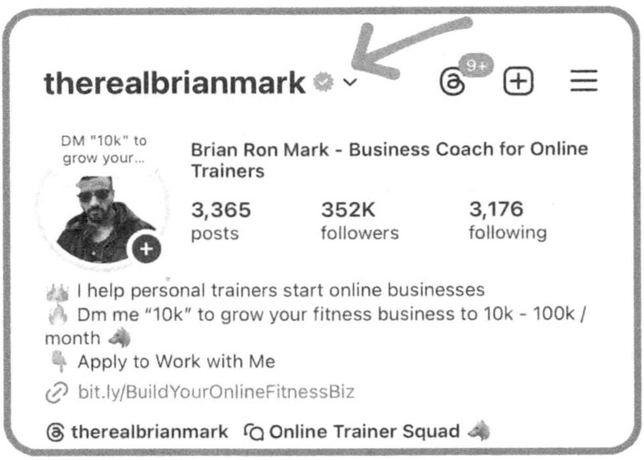

Step 2: Instagram Username

Choosing a good username might be the most important decision you make when it comes to having an online business. Your profile is your business card. This isn't one of those situations where you can say, "My business account is this," and "my personal account is this." *You* are your brand.

People don't buy from your business, they buy from you. The way you are going to turn your Instagram account into a lead generation machine is to become a personal brand that people fall in love with. That's why, when you choose an Instagram username, you have to think about a name that will attract your ideal client, that, ideally, has some form of your name in it, and that it's easily remembered.

When I was an online fitness coach, I used @bmarkfit as my Instagram username. When I decided to go all-in on my personal brand and knew I wasn't going to be a Fitness Coach forever, I created @therealbrianmark.

I'm going to give you some advice if you want to build a personal brand that makes money. Your Instagram username should be one that's easily recognizable, says what you do, and has your name attached to it in some way shape or form.

I don't think I should have to say this, but I know you might be doing this. So, take the numbers out of your name. A username like @BobSmith3344 is stupid. Act like a professional. Be one of one—not one of 3,344. Even if you want to use your favorite numbers—don't.

I also don't recommend choosing your Instagram username in an instant. Use ChatGPT to brainstorm usernames.

Try This ChatGPT Prompt

> "I am an online coach for 'specific avatar' and my Instagram username is @______. Please help me come up with ten to twenty usernames that follow these rules: easily recognizable, says what I do, and has my why attached to it in some way shape or form. My name is _______."

ChatGPT will then give you a bunch of usernames. Search each username on Instagram to see what's taken and what's available. If you find a username you like and it's already in use, ask ChatGPT to come up with ten variations of the one you like. Do this until you come across the Instagram username want to use.

Here's the thing, once you choose your username (maybe you already have one, but realize it could be better after reading this section), change it and then stick with it. You don't want to change your username every couple of months. If you do that, you'll confuse your audience and they won't know where to find you.

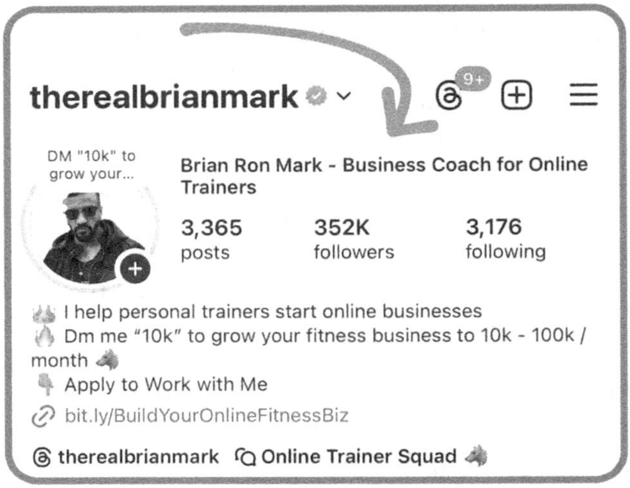

Step 3: Optimize Your Name Field

First, I want you to pay the $14.99 for Meta verification. It instantly makes you more credible. With verification, however, you will have to add your full, legal name to the name field in Instagram. But you can still make optimizations. With Meta verification, Instagram makes you use your full, legal name, but you can also add other words after your name. Mine says "Brian Ron Mark – Business Coach for Online Trainers." This is important because Instagram operates as a search engine.

When your ideal client uses Instagram to search "women's fat loss," Instagram will load results that use those specific keywords. You can use this to your advantage by adding specific keywords to your name field, so your account will rank higher in Instagram's search engine. Doing so also adds extra credibility to your bio because you can classify yourself as the No. 1 person in your field. Remember what I said at the start of this book? First you speak it, then it becomes real.

Long before I was the No. 1 business coach for online fitness coaches, I claimed that I was the No. 1 business coach for online fitness coaches—then it became my reality. So, you can use phrases like:

- Women's Fitness Expert
- Men's Fitness Expert
- Business Coach for Solar
- Mindset Coach for Dads
- No. 1 Real Estate Agent in Kelowna

Plus, when you put phrases like that in your bio, it's going to piss off your haters. To your ideal client, however, the person who's looking for the No. 1 Real Estate Agent in Kelowna, you are going to be the most reasonable and best option in their minds.

So, pay for verification and add what you do, or what you're an expert in, to the name field so you stand out from the crowd.

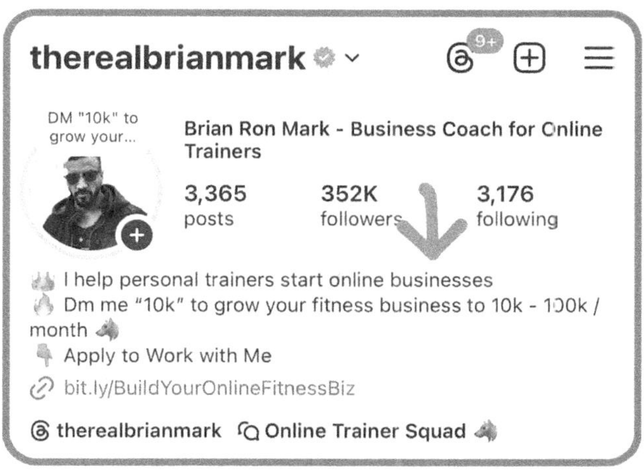

Step 4: The Tagline in Your Bio

The first thing someone is going to read when they land on your social media profile, is the tagline in your bio. For that reason, the first line in your bio needs to clearly outline why someone should follow you. More specifically, tell them what's in it for them. This is the biggest mistake online coaches make when it comes to their Instagram Profile. If you think "I want to make my bio all about me" so, you add your certifications, your credentials, and things you're proud of in your bio like "Dog Mom to Chi Chi," no one is going to care.

In fact, the only thing people care about is themselves. For that reason, you need to tell your audience why they should follow you, and you should do that in the first line in your bio.

I have a very simple formula for the first line in your bio, and I call it the "I help" statement. It reads like this: "I help [ideal client] get [specific result] in [X timeframe] without sacrificing [thing they want].

Examples

- I help busy men lose 10 pounds in 90 days with 3 workouts a week.
- I help male entrepreneurs become better leaders for their business in 6 months while making more money.
- I help online fitness coaches make 10k in their business in 6 months without spending money on ads.

The "I help" statement is something AI can help you with, too. Enter the following prompt into ChatGPT: I am an online coach for [specific avatar.] Please write twenty different variations of "I help" statements for me that I can use to post on my Instagram bio that follows this formula: I help [ideal client] person get [specific result] in [X timeframe] without sacrificing [thing they want.] I want the tagline to be punchy, and I want you to include any of your own research in terms of what you believe the most important results they'd want to accomplish are.

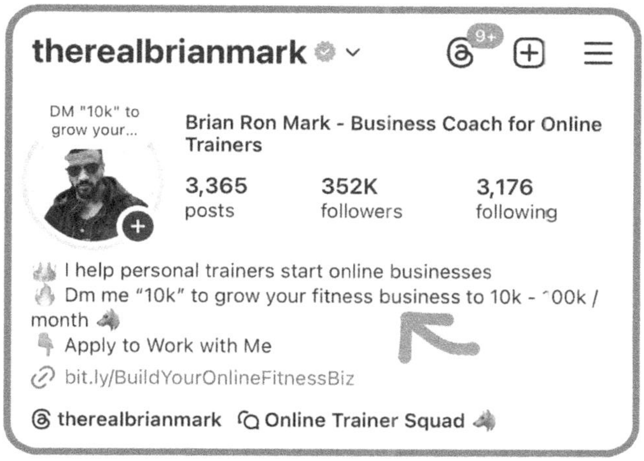

Step 5: A Clear Call to Action

Not having a clear call to action (CTA) is why most of you are not making money using Instagram. Here's the scenario: Your ideal customer finds your profile and they have no idea how to contact you for coaching. You have a Link-tree, a Link.me, or a Solo.to in your bio that links to different offers you have. The problem is that confused prospects don't buy anything. It's called choice overload, and it happens when you give a prospective client too many choices, so they choose nothing.

There's only one choice you can make when you get to my page. It's to reach out to me about coaching. Yes, I have a YouTube channel I could direct people to, and they could consume my long-form content there. Yes, I have a podcast with more than 1,200 episodes that are specifically geared toward online fitness coaches. Yes, I have an email list with more than 50,000 people I could have them subscribe to. I could use all these offerings to nurture prospective clients with lead magnets and emails. But that's not my goal for my Instagram profile. The goal for my Instagram profile is to optimize for conversions. Remember, your Instagram account *is* a marketing funnel, and in a marketing funnel you want people to opt in.

Regarding Instagram, one of the ways we get people to opt in is to have a keyword related to the dream outcome that our prospect would like to achieve. Since I am a business coach for online personal trainers, the online trainers who reach out to me all want to make a minimum of $10,000 per month with their online fitness business. So, in my bio, I say "DM me '10k' for more info." I attach a keyword for prospects to message me about coaching to an aspiration, dream, or goal that they have.

If you sell a business coaching program, think about how much money your prospects want to make. If you sell fitness, think about a keyword that your avatar uses to describe their goals. Here are a few examples:

- Toned
- Six pack
- Fit mom

If you are a photographer, think about a keyword your avatar resonates with. Maybe it's "Booking."

If you are a mindset coach, what is the core mindset you want to instill in your clients to facilitate a transformation? Maybe you use a keyword like:

- Bulletproof
- Leader
- Champion

The keyword you want prospects to DM you should be the second line in your bio and directly follow your "I help" statement.

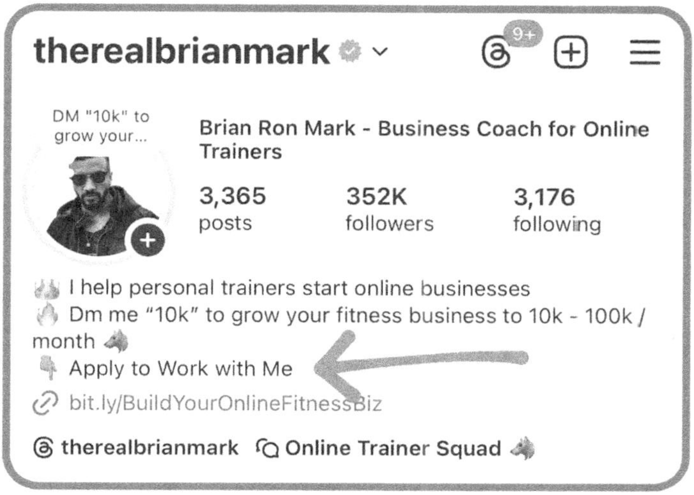

Step 6: Add the text: "Apply for Coaching" and Use an Arrow to Point to Your Clickable Link

This is a big one. Let's go back to the idea of choice overload. You want to put your Link-tree in your bio because you have so many cool and special resources for people. Don't do it.

That's why you're not making money.

You need to have one option in your bio, and it should be to work with you. Keep it simple: "Apply for coaching."

That is your goal as an online fitness coach, isn't it? To get clients? The *only* reason you'd collect a prospect's information so you could email them is so you could *eventually* warm them up to become your client. The reason you'd DM a prospect on social media is to book a call so they would hopefully become a client. The reason you post on social media is to attract people to your profile, so they consume your content and hopefully become a client. So, the most reasonable thing to do with your website link in your Instagram bio is to have a client application—and that's it. Period. Anything else in that link is a waste of time.

Figure out what offer is the most important one you have and make it your *one* link in your bio as a clickable link. Everything else is wasted space.

Yes, you can promote your YouTube, your newsletter, and your podcast. But do that with Reels, Stories, and livestreams.

Your Instagram bio is your business card, and the *only* goal of your business card is to do business. Go to Typeform.com and create a free form for your coaching program. These are the seven questions you need to ask in your form.

1. First and last name
2. Phone number
3. Email address
4. Instagram username
5. What's your No. 1 goal in [your industry] right now?
6. What's the biggest struggle you have in [your industry] right now?
7. What is your current financial situation regarding investing in a permanent solution to your problem and getting the [dream outcome you want]?
    - In the drop-down add these responses:
        - I have the funds, and I am ready and willing to invest.
        - My budget is tight, but if the program guarantees results, then I'm committed.
        - I don't really have the funds to invest in a mentor right now.
        - I just want some free advice.

This form should be the only clickable link in your bio. So, with the clickable link and the option to "DM for more information," you have two ways for prospects to contact you for coaching. The people who want to send a direct message for more information can DM your keyword and the people who are more serious about your offer will invest the time to fill out your client application. Both are good outcomes.

SUMMARY

In this section we covered exactly how to turn your Instagram bio into a business card that converts strangers on the internet into followers.

Here are the six steps again:

1. Don't blow it with your profile photo.
2. Pick a good username.
3. Optimize your name field with searchable keywords.
4. Add a "I help" tagline as the first line in your bio.
5. Add a clear CTA to the second line of your bio that tells people to DM you the keyword of your choosing.
6. Add "Apply for Coaching" as the last line of your bio and Use an Arrow emoji to point to your clickable link.

The only clickable link in your bio should be a form application for prospects to apply for coaching.

Do not move on to the next chapter until you make the changes I've outlined in this chapter. I believe in you! Let's turn your Instagram into a $10,000,000 marketing funnel.

CHAPTER 4

KNOW, LIKE AND TRUST FACTOR

"In order for people to purchase off of you, they need to know you, like you, and trust you," Gaurav Duggal told me. Gaurav was the first agency I ever hired to help me build my business. Honestly, if it wasn't for Gaurav, you wouldn't be reading this book. By the time I met Gaurav, I hit $10,000 a month for three months in a row with my online coaching business. My problem was that as I was growing the business, and the more the business grew, the more people wanted to work for me.

At that point, I traveled to Bali for three to four weeks a time and friends who were stuck working as full-time servers or as personal trainers saw the life I was living and they wanted to know how I was doing it.

If I'm being honest, I had no idea how I was doing it. I posted content at the time, every day, seven days a week, and people reached out to me and wanted to work with me. Knowing that I was building a team of personal trainers who wanted to grow their online business, I couldn't exactly say "post on social media" was the only blueprint they needed to be successful. I had to give them more information.

So, a mutual friend introduced me to Gaurav because he specialized in internet marketing. My investment to get started was $10,000. That was far beyond what I thought it would cost to get help from someone like Gaurav, but I also knew absolutely nothing about the internet marketing world. Feeling like it was my responsibility to learn more about marketing, I hired Gaurav to help me. The biggest lesson Gaurav ever taught me was that for people to purchase from you, they need to know you, like you, and trust you.

I did some research myself to find the origin of that philosophy and it can't be directly attributed to just one person. Dale Carnegie, the author of *How to Win Friends and Influence People,* wrote about building rapport and trust with people.

Bob Burg, a famous internet marketer in the 80s, wrote the book *Endless Referrals,* in which he frequently referenced the idea of being known, liked, and trusted. The known, liked, and trusted (KLT) concept is also popular in twentieth century network marketing companies.

Upon stumbling across this idea, I realized I had to devise a social media strategy around KLT. So, I came up with three content types that will help people know you, like you, and trust you. Let's look at each content type.

KNOW YOU: THE CONNECTION CONTENT

Connection content is material you share with your audience so they can get to know you. This type of content is where you share big dreams, goals, fears, struggles you've had, and what kind of animal(s) you have. It's where you share tidbits of information about your relationship with your spouse, your kids, and you share about your personal life.

This part of personal branding is fun because you get to be yourself. You share the *real* parts of you, including your authentic opinions, your outlook on controversial subjects, the way you raise your kids, and the relationship you have with your spouse.

All these pieces of information are necessary elements of creating connection content. Essentially, connection content is your audience's gateway into understanding who you are at your core. This type of content naturally convinces your audience to fall in love with you. And when your audience falls in love with you, they're more likely to do business with you.

Trent Harrison, a client of mine, is a perfect example of connection content. Trent started in my coaching program with seven thousand social media followers. He built his entire account based off his Swipe Workouts. Trent had a hard time converting his audience into his offer. When I looked at his content, I found out that he did not share *who* he was as an actual person.

For a long time, Trent attended medical school to become a doctor. He graduated with his degree and was a hop, skip, and a jump away from working as a doctor. During his time in medical school, however, Trent trained for one or two hours a day, and he filmed his gym content. He realized while he was in medical school that he wanted to be an online fitness coach and help people with their health goals *before* they ended up in the hospital. Trent thought he could make a bigger impact on people's lives by teaching them how to properly move their bodies, how to eat better, and live a healthier lifestyle so they never experienced health complications in the first place.

I knew this story, but Trent's audience didn't. So, I encouraged him to share his story and tell his audience why he started Swipe Workouts.

This was the result:

This is only a small part of Trent's story. He also is a foster father, and he brought a baby into his beautiful home. He's a man of God and holds to his core values and beliefs. Trent is also an incredible family man who puts his family first. That is the content he *wasn't* posting on social media but should have been posting all along.

We got Trent out of his shell, and he started to post content about his family, his weekends with his family, and about adopting a baby.

This is the type of content that allowed an audience to fall in love with Trent.

And the best part? He was just being himself.

The same is true for you. So, what makes you the person you are?

Think about who you are outside of business:

- What do you do for fun?
- Do you believe in God?
- What are your core values?
- What do you contribute to the community?
- Do you have kids?
- Are you married or in a relationship?

Some of my best connection content is simply relatable, funny, couples' humor posts. Because again, connection content isn't content that grows your business—it's content that's posted with the intention of your audience getting to know you.

I have a very cheeky and sarcastic sense of humor. So, I like posting content that's funny, relatable, and has nothing to do with my business. I post it with the sole intention of helping my audience get to know me on a deeper level.

Here's an example:

Now that you understand what connection content is, here are one hundred content ideas for connection-based content:

Like You: Value Content

Value content is the bread and butter of your social media. This is where most people mess up. If you post generic, boring, non-engaging, basic information, you're never going to have people throwing their cash at you.

With your ideal customer avatar, your social media is simple: to become the No. 1 trusted resource for your ideal client. Become the go-to solution for your ideal client's problem. Create content that is *so* good, *so* valuable, and *so* step by step that your ideal client has no choice but to follow you, save your content, comment, engage, share it with their friends, and watch it again.

That's the deciding factor in whether someone sees you as the solution to their problem.

The BMARK definition of value content is: Content that is so good that your ideal client can get results for free without hiring you.

That's why many of you are reading this book. You found my social media content, heard me on a podcast, watched my YouTube videos, and through consuming my content you were able to take an action that benefited your business in some way.

That's the goal you need to have. Help your audience get results in advance of hiring you. Now how do you make this happen?

Figure out *exactly* what your ideal client is struggling with and create specific solutions to their problems.

I'll give you an example: I'm a business coach for online personal trainers. In my industry my clients struggle with posting on social media. Let's go deeper.

My clients struggle with feeling awkward on camera. They struggle with writing content scripts. They struggle with coming up with hook ideas. They struggle with being consistent on social media. They struggle with imposter syndrome on social media.

So, I can take any one of those problems and I can create a piece of value content that specifically solves one of those problems for them.

Let's pretend we're going to talk about helping my audience develop hook ideas.

I'd start by creating a piece of social media content that included a step-by-step formula to help them create better hooks.

First, I need to ask myself: Does my audience understand what a hook is?

The average reading level in the United States is at the fifth grade reading level, so I'm going to assume that my audience doesn't know what a hook is.

I'll start my content by defining what a hook is and why it's important on social media. Once I explain that, I'll assume I need to teach my audience how to structure a hook and what to put in the hook to make it actionable enough for their audience to be able to do something with. Next, I'll likely share some specific words they can use in their hooks to grab people's attention and make them want to watch the entire video. Finally, I'll share in my post something that's relatable for my audience. This means I'll talk about what they're likely doing wrong in their current hooks.

In summary, I need to create a piece of content that explains what a hook is, why it's important, and why all great videos need a great hook. I'm also going to tell my clients what they're doing wrong with their current hooks, and then I'm going to give them something actionable to that they can do right away.

Here's how I'd write the script:

> The reason your videos get no views is because your hooks are boring. Most of you start your video saying "Here's three tips to help you lose weight."
>
> That's boring.
>
> Your audience just scrolled away from your video.
>
> Unless you grab someone's attention in the first three seconds of a video, they're just going to scroll past your content, which will negatively impact your watch time and your video's engagement.
>
> Instead, grab their attention in the first three seconds by saying something negative or telling them something they're doing wrong.
>
> Use words like:
>
> - Stop
> - Steal
> - Don't
> - Avoid

> Or tell them something they're screwing up. I promise you, your videos are going to get a lot more views.

That video will convince your audience members to save the video so they can refer to it later. They are going to send it to their friends, leave a comment, or even watch the video again to grasp the full concept. It's value content that's so good your ideal client can get results without paying you. If you do that enough your audience is going to start to like you, which is an important element in whether they're willing to buy in to your coaching program.

Here's a simple exercise to determine whether your content on social media is valuable or not. I want you to go to your Instagram profile right now and scroll through your most recent nine posts. Then I want you to think about your ideal client demographic.

Ask yourself: If my ideal client found my page right now and started consuming content with the most recent nine posts, would they be able to take action and start seeing positive results in their life?

If your answer is "no," you'll immediately understand why your content isn't performing well and why people aren't following, sharing, liking, commenting or telling their friends about your page.

The ideal piece of value content is one that gives step-by-step, actionable value. Think about a cooking video for example. The best cooking videos are the ones that walk you through the exact process of how to make the recipe. Let's take that same concept and apply it to sales coaching. You may need to post a step-by-step video on "When someone says, 'I need to talk to my wife,' here's exactly what you say" to overcome the "wife objection" on a call.

That's value content.

You need to give a specific solution to a narrowly defined problem, and your solution needs to be shared in a step-by-step format.

Let's take the cooking video idea and apply it to mindset coaching now. You'd need to post a step-by-step video on how to decrease your anxiety when it creeps up suddenly in public settings.

Your value should always be packaged as a step by step.

Here are twenty-five value content ideas for five niches, including health, sales, business, content, and mindset coaching:

In the next chapter, I will teach you exactly how to structure these ideas and give them viral packaging, but for now you at least understand the definition of value content, and I've given you some ideas to play with as a place to start.

Take this information and insert your own expert advice. Once you identify what your audience struggles with, it's up to you to create solutions that are so good they get results for free. Only then will they start to like you.

PROOF: TRUST YOU

This is the single most important piece of content that you need to post if you want to sign clients. Everyone's an expert these days. Everyone knows what they're talking about. Everyone's posting tip videos. But who has the proof to back up what they're saying?

Proof content is simple; it's content that demonstrates evidence that you followed your own advice.. The first part of proof that we need to discuss is *you*. You are the proof. You should be the walking, talking, billboard for success in your industry. If you're not, you need to be. Don't be the fitness coach who doesn't work on their goals. Don't be the mindset coach who has crippling anxiety. Don't be the business coach who failed at building their own business. Don't be the content coach with five thousand Instagram followers. Don't be the sales coach who can't sell to save his life.

Become an expert in your field because as soon as you become an expert and you walk, breathe and are a living example of what your advice looks like in its full form—it's *very* easy to document proof.

Think about someone like Wes Watson. Whether you love or hate the guy, he is walking proof. He's jacked year-round. He's rich as hell. He buys a new supercar every month. Regardless of your opinion about Wes Watson or not, the guy is a walking billboard of social proof. He is living *that* life.

You don't need to be tatted, jacked, and rich to be successful on social media. But if you're a sales coach, why not record some calls where you're closing deals? That's proof real fast! If you're a content coach, why not break down one of your most recent viral Instagram Reels and tell people how you did it? If you're a fitness coach, why not show your own weight-loss transformation and what you do on a day-to-day basis to stay in great shape?

Be the example. Walk the talk. That's the easiest way to show social proof. That's also the best way to show proof if you have zero clients. Why? Because if clients follow your advice, they'll get the results you have.

I can't tell you how many people try to skip this step. There are fitness coaches who look like bags of milk and wonder why aren't signing clients. Content coaches who have ten thousand Instagram followers try to sell a course on how to go viral. Financial advisors who have only one thousand dollars in their bank account try to tell you what you should put your money into.

Walk the walk, then show you living that life and give people an example to follow. You don't need to be perfect, but you *do* need to walk the walk. Then you can post your own story as your social proof. It's easy to demonstrate the effects of listening to your own advice if you actually take your own advice.

Get in shape.

Be good at sales.

Be good at content.

Become an expert in your field then you can talk about your success. This is why it took me *so damn long* to write this book. I had enough success in my field to be an expert, but I knew I needed to have a stack of evidence piled up me to give me credibility to come to you with business growth information.

I walk the talk. I've had $30,000,000 in sales in six years. Eighty percent of those sales came through Instagram. That's *definitely* enough evidence to tell you how you can make money on Instagram.

What else can you do?

Happy clients are the best type of proof. When your clients are happy because they're getting great results inside your container—that's what's going to attract high-ticket clients who are willing to pay a premium price.

Show what happens when clients listen to your advice. Another part you need to know is that people follow other people's social behaviors. We're herd animals, so when people can see you are already working with people, that means others have already trusted you with their money, more people are likely to trust you because trust carried over from people who already made the decision to work with you.

Now, I'm going to give you the most basic advice on proof, and you're going to feel like you already know it. And I'm going to challenge you with this: If you already knew it, why isn't it baked into your social media strategy?

I'm talking about before and after transformations. We're not just talking about before and after photos though, which can be a powerful representation of transformation. What about before and after videos? You can show a client before they worked with you, and that client after they started working with you. What about before and after stories? You can talk about a specific message a client sent to you before they worked with you and you can share a message they just sent you last week. What about before and after interviews? Get a client on a livestream and you talk about their experience in your coaching container. What about before and after case study videos? Do a longer form piece of content in which you explain where a client was when they first started with you and discuss the exact advice you gave them and the results that came from that.

All of these before and after examples are social proof.

In one sentence, in relation to social proof that isn't you waking the talk, you need to show evidence of successful clients who are currently working with you.

You can do this in a variety of ways, and some already listed above. Here are five more suggestions:

- Screenshots of client wins
- Screenshots of comments in your client group
- Screenshots of any sort of key performance indicators (KPIs) you use to track client data (weight, income, closing %)
- Testimonial videos sent a client has sent to you
- Photos of clients when they started versus where they are now

This needs to be a pillar in your content strategy. If you don't have social proof, you don't have a business. People are going to pay you based off the transformation that you are able to take them through. Unless you can demonstrate examples of specific transformations that have come as a specific result of taking your advice, you're not going to get many people who want to pay you their hard-earned money.

Now, there's freedom in this advice. All you need to do to successfully integrate social proof into your content is to walk the walk. Beyond that, you'll attract your first few rounds of clients. Once you have a few clients, all you have to do is not suck and document the journey of their transformation. Then, you'll be able to share successful client stories of people who followed your advice.

"How do I get more social proof?" You ask.

This is a question I get every day. Here's a simple piece of advice. If you're brand new and just getting started, work for free. I teach my clients how to run successful "14 Day Free Challenges." Inside of this container, they give participants everything they would typically give them if they'd paid for a full coaching program, and at the end of fourteen days those participants are able to see visible results and most often they want to continue. From conversion events such as that, your average conversion rate will be about 20%. So, if you have twenty people participate in a fourteen-day challenge and they all complete it—you can expect four new clients.

It's not just about the clients you're going to sign at the end of the challenge, however, it's also about the fact that you'll have twenty people who will have documented, transformative stories you can use in your content.

How to Ask for a Testimonial Video

When you have a client in your container who's getting great results, or loves working with you, send them a message that says:

> **You:** Hey [Name], I have a question and it might seem weird, but do you enjoy working with me?
>
> Them: Of course I do! (Hopefully, you don't suck, and this is what they'll say.)
>
> You: That's amazing! Can you film a quick, 60–90 second testimonial video for my business? It doesn't have to be long or professional, or anything like that. You can just answer these three questions:

1: What were your hesitations joining the program?

2: What are the specific results we've gotten as we've worked together?

3: Would you recommend me to others as your coach?

Thanks so much for your help with this!

Just like that, you'll start to get more testimonial videos you can use for social media marketing.

SUMMARY

For people to purchase from you, they need to know you, they need to like you, and they need to trust you. To create the know, like, trust (KLT) effect with your social media marketing efforts, you need to create three types of content. They are connection, value, and proof content.

Connection content allows your audience to get to know you on a deeper level. You let them in and show them your beliefs, values, and adversities, as well as your wins, and who you are as a person. This will help your audience get to know you.

To get your audience to like you, you'll create value content. My definition of value content is content that is so good your audience can get results for free without hiring you. I hope this book is that for you —content that's so good you can get results for free without hiring me. When you create this content enough, your audience will grow to like you.

Finally, to get your audience to trust you, proof content is key. You need to show your audience evidence of what it's like to follow and listen to your advice. You need to give practical, real-world examples of people who have gone through your coaching program, taken your advice, and achieved amazing results. Most importantly, though, you have to walk the walk. When you become a walking billboard for success and people can see the success in your industry just by looking at you—I promise your income will immediately increase, and sales will effortlessly come to you.

CHAPTER 5

THE ANATOMY OF A VIRAL INSTAGRAM REEL

You worked hard on your post. You scripted it, aimed it directly at your avatar, you spoke well during the video, you added captions, you used trending audio, and you made sure to put a cover photo on the Reel.

You anxiously wait to see what the result of your hard work will be, excited for the internet to consume your valuable piece of content and rave about it to all their friends. You leave your phone for ten minutes then check to see how your Reel is performing. Fifty views. What? All that hard work on one piece of content, and it has fifty views!

You think, "Maybe it's getting more likes than views." So, you check the like count—two likes.

Damnit.

We all know that feeling too well. The feeling of posting on social media and getting absolutely no engagement even though you tried your best to put out a good piece of content. That's why most people fail at social media. They're too focused on the micro and not focused on the macro.

In this chapter, we're going to go deep into the mindset you need to go viral. I'm also going to give you what you need to consistently go viral. I will break down the anatomy of a viral

Instagram Reel and I'll help you understand the elements that make an Instagram Reel explode.

By the end of this chapter, you will be armed with the tools to go viral and you'll be fired up and motivated to tackle the challenge head on.

In November 2021, my Instagram account was disabled. I was on a vacation in Mexico with my wife, and during the trip I logged onto Instagram and a notification said, "Your account has been permanently disabled."

I used that account to build my fitness business, and I transitioned it to business coaching content. I had 100,000 followers on that account. If I'm being honest though, I participated in two celebrity giveaways at one point. That means, I paid a middle man who connected me to Lil Baby's giveaway. Lil Baby posted on his account, "I'm giving away two iPhones and five thousand dollars cash to one of my followers. All you have to do to enter is follow everyone I'm following."

So, fifty people, like myself, who paid to be part of the giveaway all gained 10,000 to 20,000 followers based on people who hoped to win Lil Baby's giveaway.

As the giveaway was awarded, all those people who followed you either unfollowed you because they didn't care about you or never engaged with your content because they didn't care about you.

My engagement on that account was sub-par at best due to that giveaway. I was lucky if I got three- to five-thousand views on my Reels with an account following of 100,000. Despite the poor engagement on my account, I built an extremely loyal audience.

With that account, I enrolled up to 120 clients a month. Losing that account was a major business problem. As soon as I got the notification, I immediately tried to appeal it and got in contact with Meta. I even paid someone who had a contact at Meta $15,000 to get my account up and active again. I spent twenty-four hours trying to get my account active. I didn't sleep. That Instagram account was the main source of my business income and it disappeared in an instant.

At the time, I didn't have the awareness to build an email list on the back end with ads or to use a sell-by-text system—both of which I've since developed.

After forty-eight hours trying to get my account back I decided to start a new account @therealbrianmark. I also told myself I wasn't going to cut corners. I decided that I was going to post twice a day, seven days a week, and that I'd never miss a day. Luckily, my podcast had 100,000 downloads a month. So, I told my podcast audience about my new account and pretty quickly gained followers.

Everything else was a slow burn. I went from one hundred sales a month to forty. I was used to a low view count, but that didn't seem to bother me because I didn't have the follower count behind me.

So, I maintained my new posting schedule. Truth be told, I don't think I was a great content creator until that happened. With my old account, I had no idea if a piece of my content was good because my engagement was poor, so it was hard to determine what the algorithm actually wanted. I got rewarded when I posted *good* content.

Starting a new Instagram account allowed me to become a student of the game and study my own content. And let me tell you—it was humbling. I got one thousand views on most of the videos I posted during that time. That was the pattern for months. I think that's why most people fail—they give up because they don't see results. Not only do you need to be consistent, but you also need to be good. Unless you're a good content creator, you're going to consistently post bad content.

Consistency then Quality

I spent two years following a consistent posting schedule. I also spent hundreds of thousands of dollars to gain access to the best content creation mentors. I hired Devin Jhato to help me with content scripts, ideation, and video editing. I paid close to $10,000 a month for his service, and I worked with him for up to a year. Devin was ruthless. He ripped apart my content.

The content that I thought was good, he made me realize the reason my content didn't going viral was because it sucked. Devin is a genius.

After working with Devin, I met Adley Kinsman. She gets billions of views across all the accounts she manages. Adley is the Marketing Director for First Phorm and she's has her own company, Viralish, in which she helps creators go viral.

Adley gave me three options to work with her:

1. $15,000 for group coaching for $15,000
2. $50,0000 for one-on-one coaching with one of her coaches
3. $100,000 for six months of one-on-one coaching with her

I chose the third option and paid $100,000 because I wanted to directly work with Adley. It was the best decision I ever made.

In this chapter, I'm going to break down the lessons I learned from some of the best content creators I've worked with. I also want to simplify what I learned and insert my own expert advice.

Let's start with the concept of consistency first, then quality, then volume.

You need to be consistent with social media, first. My definition of consistency is posting five to seven times a week. It takes zero time to post on the weekend. It's not hard to post, but you have to be consistent. Once you can be consistent for one-hundred days, then you'll focus on quality.

We're going to focus on quality in this chapter, and I'm going to give you a step-by-step formula so you understand the anatomy of a viral Instagram Reel.

TWO DIFFERENT TYPES OF REELS

From a macro perspective, the three content types are connection, proof, and value. Beyond that, when you create content, you'll create one of two content styles, which are awareness and conversion content.

Awareness content is designed to get you in front of millions of people. Conversion content is designed to turn your audience into paying clients.

Awareness Content

The reason we label this content style "awareness" is because it's used to get in front of a wider audience. With awareness content, you need to think about how can we keep strangers who don't know you on the platform for longer and spread awareness for your business. To do that, you need to be relatable to a larger audience. When you are relatable to a larger audience, as you choose to be with awareness content, your content will get pushed to a larger number of people. Fifty percent of your content strategy should be awareness-based content.

I'll give you an example. If you are a fitness coach for moms who have twenty or more pounds to lose, then the moms who have weight to lose is the narrow niche. You can broaden that niche if you make a video for women. Half of the population is women. You could also make a video for moms? I don't know how many moms there are in the world, but there's a lot.

So, your awareness content is made for a wider audience, but still feeds your demographic. That way, you can cast a wider net and bring more people into your world.

I will caution this, while awareness content is more widely relatable, you don't want to be widely relatable to *everyone.* If you're a fitness coach for moms who have weight to lose and you want to widen your net to reach more women who might be interested in your offer, you *aren't* going to be successful if you post videos of you shooting wild animals for sport. Most likely, those videos will attract the wrong type of audience. More than likely, those videos would attract a bunch of men because they'll think the woman in the videos is cool.

Women who want to lose twenty pounds can be your niche focus, but you can also make videos that speak to women in general. To do this, could post content about being a woman versus a man. Instill some humor, too. Maybe a Reel about when it's that time of the month and everything he says annoys you. That would be a great piece of awareness content. Women will comment, "Oh my god, yes!"

To reach a wider audience, create content that's relatable to a wider audience but also still includes your niche.

The goal of awareness content is to be seen by a wider audience—not convert clients. So, when you create awareness content, your information doesn't have to be valuable.

There are several ways to trigger your followers' emotions, but from personal experience the best way to do so in a way that doesn't affect your mental health is to make them laugh.

Sure, you could make them angry. You could make them sad. You could even make them hate you. It's actually easy to make them hate you; just start a video with "Fat parents are disgusting and should be ashamed of themselves."

I'll bet you that video gets a lot of views! I also guarantee that video negatively affects your mental health and makes you question yourself because the internet will come for you.

That's why I believe the best approach to awareness content is through humor.

Conversion Content

Conversion content gives people step-by-step information that offers a ton of value. Take the information that's in your head and translate it into a simpler language for your audience to understand. You know what you want to say to your audience. So, don't overcomplicate it by adding fancy words to make you sound smart. If you do that, you'll just confuse your audience.

CHAPTER 5

Let's discuss how to come up with different topics to discuss in your conversion content, so you know exactly what you're going to talk about. Start macro with your subjects, then go micro to get your content pillars.

Let's start with macro subjects.

Say you're a fitness coach for women who want to lose weight. Think about the different aspects of weight-loss that are important to this subject? You'll likely say:

- Exercise
- Nutrition
- Mindset
- Recovery

That now gives us four macro subjects you can discuss. Within these macro subjects, you'll need to get specific.

For the macro topic of exercise, you would get micro topics by asking yourself:

- What are the biggest struggles women who want to lose weight have with exercise?
- What does their workout plan usually look like?
- What are some beliefs they have about exercise that are not true?
- How many times a week are they currently exercising?
- Are there any parts of their body they're hoping to improve with exercising?
- What are some of the frustrations they have with going to the gym?
- Have they tried an exercise plan before and failed?

Dissect your other three content pillars—nutrition, mindset, and recovery—the same way. Then, brainstorm digestible, bite-sized problems you can solve for your ideal client based off your four content pillars.

To make the content brainstorming process easier, use ChatGPT to answer this prompt: I'm an online fitness coach for women who have twenty pounds to lose. I'm looking for content ideas to help this woman out. Can you please help me come up with twenty different content ideas specifically related to exercise? Include the most-asked questions on the internet, as well as common struggles they face.

You'll instantly get twenty content ideas that are related to exercise.

Do this for all four macro pillars of your ideal customer journey to get unlimited content ideas.

Knowing the purpose of conversion content, and what you are going to talk about is important, but it's not enough. You have to learn how to take those ideas from ChatGPT and turn them into viral pieces of content.

THE ANATOMY OF A VIRAL INSTAGRAM REEL

You know how to create content pillars and brainstorm content ideas for those pillars, so now you need to know how to make your content go viral once you post it. This involves the following formula:

Scroll stopping hook + Personality + Step-by-Step Value + CTA=Viral Instagram Reel

Scroll Stopping Hook

Let's start with the scroll stopping hook. The hook is the opening three seconds of your video.

In this short window of time, you need to captivate your viewers so much that they want to watch your video.

Most of my content (80–90%) uses a negative hook; negativity is polarizing. It's why you instantly slow down when you drive by a car crash—you want to see what's happening. It's also why every news headline is over the top dramatic.

Yet, when we see a mother and daughter out for a walk, holding hands, we never think twice and go on with our lives.

We can't help it, we are drawn to negativity. It captures our attention. It makes us want to watch. Love it or hate it, negativity always grabs people's attention.

I'm not encouraging you to be negative in your content. In fact, I want you to get so much value for free from my page that you never have to hire me because you get crazy good results from watching my content.

For you to receive my value, however, I must deliver it in a way that grabs your attention.

Value is based on perception. So, let's examine what it takes to produce an attention-grabbing hook that stops your audience in their tracks and makes them want to pay attention.

Three hook types exist: the extra-ordinary, draws on pain or negativity to trigger you, or uses humor.

Extra-Ordinary Hooks

Let's first discuss hooks that are extraordinary, or extremely positive. I say "extra-ordinary" because you need to give your audience a reason to pay attention to your information. Personally, the extra-ordinary hook isn't my favorite, but I use it every so often because it's effective.

Here are a few examples:

> Ordinary: Here's how to close your next sales call.
>
> Extra-ordinary: I've closed more than $30,000,000 in sales and this one secret changed everything for me.
>
> Ordinary: My client, Mina's, testimonial.
>
> Extra-ordinary: My client, Mina, went from $20,000 to $40,000 a month in 90 days!

You can also do hooks that are extremely positive.
Positivity Example:

> Original: This secret will help you close more sales calls.
>
> Positive: This Sales secret is *so* good it should be illegal!

I like using this hook style when I'm post social proof content.

Hooks that Draw on Pain or Negativity

My personal favorite hooks to use are hooks that draw on pain or negativity to create a trigger. This is the most effective hook style I've found that consistently produces results for myself, and my clients. I also believe this hook style is why I gained 200,000 followers in eighteen months.

Here's the simple formula you need to remember: Take all of your "How to" videos and rewrite them into "Don't do" videos.

Here's an example:

> How to: Explain to your audience how to do a squat
>
> Don't do: Never do your squats like this! You'll ruin your back."

That will get your follower's attention *and* you can tell them exactly how to do a squat.

All that led to that simple twist in content delivery was asking yourself:

- What are the mistakes my audience makes regarding [X] subject?
- What is the pain my audience experiences in relation to [X] subject?

- What is my audience struggling with in regard to [X] subject?

If you're talking about the right information, but your content isn't getting a ton of views try this hook style.

Ask yourself what the best part of the video is, then put it at the beginning of your video. You need to make sure your hook is *so* good that people must stop and watch your content.

You might piss them off, you might trigger them, or you might push them to disagree with you, but you need to grab their attention in the opening three seconds of your Reel or your content won't go viral.

Hooks that Use Humor to Break the Pattern

This is my runner-up favorite hook style. In another life, if I were a comedian, I'd use humor hooks to break the pattern. When it comes to content creation, however, if you're the funny guy, that's cool. You made me laugh, but I'm not going to pay you thousands of dollars to solve my problem. You can, however, use humor to break the pattern, which can be an effective way to start a video.

Here's an easy rule you can follow that will make your hooks more humorous and valuable. This is something I also teach my clients who struggle to find their humor. The rule is: exaggerate.

I think exaggeration is the easiest way to use humor to break the pattern. My client, Anthony Anisimov, used it in his content. When Anthony first came to me, he was the boring tip guy who told you how to gain more muscle on social media. My team helped him hit $10,000 a month, but that's where he remained. His content stalled and had no idea how to break through the plateau. We audited his content and realized that he was boring.

"Yeah, but guys, that's just my personality," Anthony said. "I'm not a loud guy."

I'll give you the advice we gave Anthony. Be entertaining. Exaggerate. Even if you're not the "funny person," treat it like gametime when you hit the record button. Put on your entertainer face. Every famous person does the same thing.

Selena Gomez during an interview versus Selena Gomez at home on a Friday hanging out with her fiancé—two completely different people.

Not *all* of your content needs to be extra, but when you get on the "stage" that is social media you need to perform.

ADD PERSONALITY

I want you to think about the last time you had a good laugh with a friend. What did you laugh about? Now, as yourself why you can give that version of yourself to your friends, but you can't bring it to social media. You need to add your personality to your content!

Talk to social media as if your followers are your friends. This will help you build relationships with your audience.

If you're wondering, "But Brian, how do I add personality to my videos?"

That's a great question. How do you bring your personality to your dating life? To your friendships? To your relationships with your kids?

You just *do*.

You don't try in those situations; you just *have* a personality. It's the same for social media. Don't try—just be personable.

I know it's hard to do that with a camera pointed at you, but that's just you being nervous and not wanting to film. Remember what I said about one hundred dirty reps? Your only goal right now is to crank out one hundred consistent pieces of content. The more you film and the most your post, the more you'll loosen up and allow your personality to come through.

In your first one hundred pieces of content, just practice. Start to joke around, laugh, and have fun with your scripts. You have to get to a point where you are comfortable enough to joke around and be playful on camera. *Personality* is the true secret sauce.

STEP BY STEP VALUE

Step-by-step value is *easy*. Take the valuable information you have in your head and deliver it to your audience in a step-by-step format. There are two ways to approach value in your content. You can do overarching value, which means your give step-by-step value on a system. You can also do narrowly defined value, which means you give a specific solution to a narrowly defined problem.

Here's an example of overarching value: The four main objections you're going to get are time, spouse, money and "I'll think about it." In this video, I'm going to break down how to overcome every one of them.

Here's an example of narrowly defined value: A talking track on how to overcome the wife objection.

Both value pieces have their place, and one is not better than the other. In fact, they both can be extremely effective.

Here's how you can mess it up:

1. You're too broad and generic, which means you don't provide any value your followers can *actually use*.
2. You overexplain yourself, which makes your content boring because you essentially say the same thing three times in your video.

Let me break down the ideal way to create value content, and we'll use the "How to Overcome the Wife Objection" example.

A talking track is a good value for this objection because you can share how you'd handle the conversation. Here's the example script for a talking track:

Oh, you need to speak to your wife? That's not a problem. I typically run major decisions through my spouse as well. Does your wife know we're speaking today?

Your prospect will say "yes." That means you can respond with, "That's perfect. And typically speaking, is she supportive of your goals? She wants you to win?"

An example of bad value content is telling your audience, "Prospects will give you the wife objection because it's a smoke screen. They're afraid of commitment. So, you need to call the prospect out on the call because if they leave the phone without paying you, it's highly likely you won't close the deal."

See the difference in the two examples? The first example *actually* tells the audience what to say when the wife objection comes up. That's good value. Sure, the second example seems good because *technically* it's right. However, it's not good enough to convince your audience to save the video.

If you want to post about your morning routine, share three things that make an effective morning routine and give your audience the tools and resources they can use to make their mornings easier.

Instead of posting about how to be more positive, share an affirmation your audience can say every day or share a morning or evening ritual they can use to work on their positivity.

Don't simply talk about weight loss in your content, instead give your followers a step-by-step plan to help them lose twenty pounds in ninety days. Give them the tools and resources they can use immediately to get results.

All of these examples show how to provide value without being boring.

The more value that you give, the better.

When you write your scripts for value content, write them in a step-by-step format. I like to do step by step, provide a specific talking track, or offer a specific tool or resource to use. Then, if

I do give that tool and resource, a step-by-step plan to actually get the most out of that tool or resource.

Here's how to practice writing value content. I want you to get all the information out of your head and written down first. I'll show you how.

Let's use the example of a calorie deficit to lose weight.

> If you want to lose weight, you need to be in a calorie deficit. Most people think they have health issues, hormone issues, or big bones, but the reality is that you pick up the fork too much. For weight loss to occur, you need to be in a deficit of five hundred calories a day, which means that you need to be eating less food than your body uses for energy. When you do this right, you'll lose weight.

You'll notice that material isn't in step-by-step format. So, what can we do with this information to make it step by step? We can teach followers how to figure out their ideal calories. Here's how we'd revise our content:

> If you want to lose weight, you need to be in a calorie deficit. Most people think they have health issues, hormone issues, or big bones, but the reality is that you pick up the fork too much. For weight loss to occur, you need to be in a calorie deficit. That means you need to eat less food then your body uses for energy. To figure out your maintenance calories, take your bodyweight in pounds and multiply it by 15. For example, 200 pounds multiplied by 1.5 = 3,000 calories. To be in a deficit to lose weight, I recommend subtracting 500 calories, which would put you at an intake of 2,500 calories a day.

Now, with the step by step formula, we need to make it short and punchy. To do this, we'd paste the text into ChatGPT and ask it to rewrite the script to make it shorter, punchier, and to add humor. The version ChatGPT gives us is our baseline script for our value content.

From there, we'd add a scroll stopping hook, and our personality, and we'd teach our audience how to be in a calorie deficit.

CALL TO ACTION (CTA)

You need to call your audience to act on every video you post. The reason for this is you never know which video will go turbo viral. If you have a video go turbo viral and it has no CTA attached, you're going to be pissed.

Trust me, I was.

Be careful with your CTAs because Instagram's algorithm is looking for watch time, which means It's looking at the total percentage of your videos that people watch. So, if people watch a lower percentage of your videos, that means Instagram will not push your content. That's why we take the video scripts we write and we make them shorter and punchier. Long, drawn out explanations that don't need to be in our videos will cause our audience to scroll away from our content and not pay attention.

That's why your CTA should be short, sexy, and straight to the point at the end of your video.

The best CTAs are often:

- Follow for more value.
- Follow for a no B.S. sales approach.
- Leave a comment if this was valuable.

The level two ninja, however, is to include your CTAs in your content, meaning you bake it into your scripts.

Example: When someone says, "I need to talk to my wife," here's what you say. And you should probably save this video, because I'm going to put you on some game.

You need to have a CTA in every video *except* funny content. Putting a CTA on funny content or awareness-based, top of the funnel content feels weird to me. But when you post value content, you must always add a CTA to your content.

SUMMARY

In this chapter, you learned about the two types of content you can post: awareness and conversion content. Awareness-based content is designed to get you in front of a wider audience. Conversion-based content is designed to turn followers into buyers.

I also broke down the anatomy of a viral Instagram Reel, and I gave you some real advice on how to structure your content so it goes viral. This includes:

Scroll stopping hook + Personality + Step-by-Step Value + CTA = Viral content

In the next chapter, I'm going to share exactly how to write content scripts, batch record your content, and how to edit your videos like a pro.

CHAPTER 6

THE LAWS OF BATCHING, RECORDING, AND EDITING

So, you want to be famous? You want your content to pop off and be seen by hundreds of thousands (maybe even millions) of people every month? If that's the case, you need to have a system. It's not enough to post occasionally and hope your content goes viral; you must be methodical in your approach.

Before we can talk about how to be consistent with your content schedule, let's talk about how to develop a process that systematically produces high quality content. We're going to break this chapter into 3 separate categories:

1. Batching Your Scripts
2. Batch Recording Your Content
3. Batch Editing Your Content

Scripting Your Content

This is the biggest struggle most people have regarding content creation. They don't know how to write scripts. We briefly discussed how you should structure your content scripts in the previous chapter, and in this chapter, I'm going to break it down even further and give you a process you can steal and use right away to get results.

Before you script, you need to come up with the idea. Ideation for me is half the battle when it comes generating viral content ideas. For this, you can do two forms of ideation. The first is creation based off information you have and know your avatar will get value from. The second is content research, which is content based off what other creators have already proven to go viral. When you first get started, you're going to get a lot more viral content ideas by doing content research.

You don't know what you're doing when you first start out, so the way to get around that is to find viral creators who are in your niche and produce content that is going viral. Then steal like an artist from them.

Good artists copy; great artists steal. Here's the process to do content research.

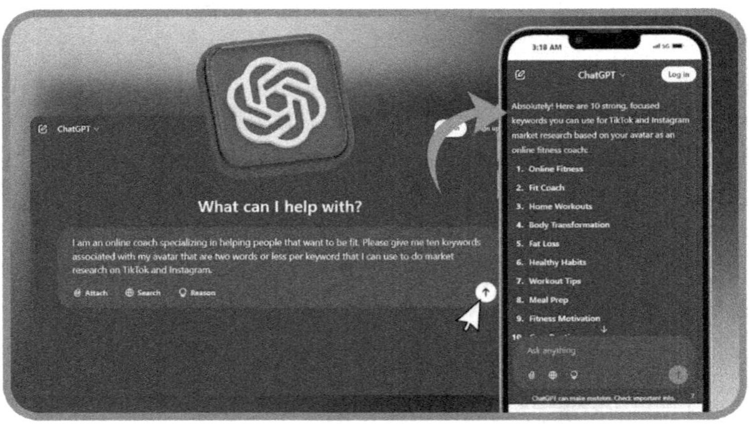

First, identify the keywords associated with your niche that you're going to search. To do this, use ChatGPT and this prompt: I am an online coach specializing in helping [X] avatar. Please give me ten keywords associated with my avatar that are two words or less per keyword that I can use to do market research on TikTok and Instagram.

Next, type the keywords into the TikTok and Instagram search bars.

After you do that, sort by best performing Reels, which are the Reels that have more than 100,000 views.

Circle Reels with 100,000+ views

You can steal that idea itself or you can visit the creator's account. To do so, tap on the account for the creator who posted the Reel. Once on their account, go to Viralfindr.com and type in their username.

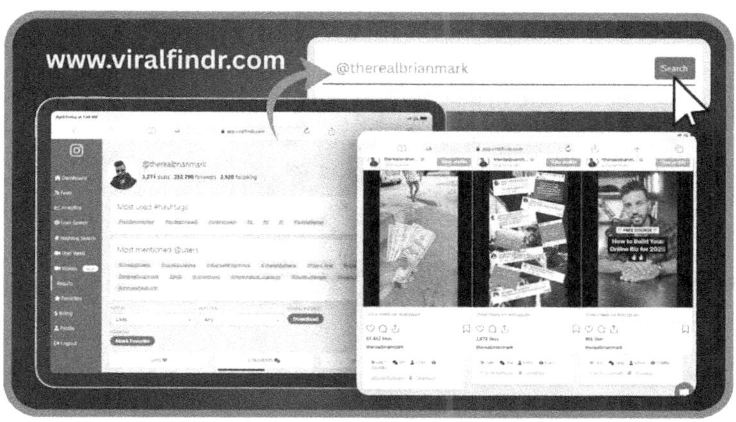

Viralfindr will load that account's best performing content. Once you see their highest performing content, you can start stealing, including their hooks.

Sometimes the words people say, the way they say things, the props they use, the way they set up the camera, or the setting they use is why the video went viral. Something about that specific subject matter, however, resonated with your ideal client, so you can steal the subject matter. You can also steal the video format. Was it a split screen video, a whiteboard video, a selfie style video talking to the camera? You can steal that, too.

Whatever you do—don't plagiarize. Meaning, don't copy other people's content word-for-word and shot-for-shot. Your goal is to steal either the hook, the subject matter, the method of delivery, the or props used in the video, then insert your expert advice into your own video.

After you do your initial research, you're going to copy the specific link to that video and paste it into your Notes app in your phone. You're going to repeat this process until you have ten to fifteen viral video ideas you can pull inspiration from.

Ideation for Scripting: 60 Minutes

Once you complete your ideation for scripting, it's time to write your scripts. To help you, I've included five templates you can use.

SCRIPT 1

SCRIPT 2

SCRIPT 3

SCRIPT 4

These templates were designed to give you a baseline for your content, but these are only training wheels. Feel free to use these templates as cheat sheets and then start writing your own content scripts based off the formulas provided in this book. This is when you'll really step into your power as a creator.

When you sit down to write scripts, watch the viral video and decide what you're going to steal.

Let's say you steal the hook. Use the same hook in your video, almost verbatim, but then insert your own expert advice. Put your own value-based information in your content after you deliver the hook.

If you want to steal the subject matter of a video, such as talking about overcoming the wife objection, do that but put your own creative spin on your video. Add an attention-grabbing hook that stops the scroll and make people want to pay attention.

My favorite way of stealing like an artist, however, is taking a concept someone else delivered, (let's say a whiteboard video) and you deliver the same information in a split screen video format where you talk to yourself.

When you write your scripts, you want to batch them all at one time. So, you'll sit down and write all your content scripts at one time. It's going to take you 60–120 minutes to write your content scripts all at once. The first couple are going to be challenging, but writing will get easier as you continue. You'll get into a flow state, and once you're in a flow state it's a lot easier to get your content done.

Your goal is to get at least seven scripts done. Because seven scripts is equivalent to one piece of content every day for one week.

I write twenty to thirty scripts at once, but I also post six times a day. It's very time consuming, but I get it done. So, if I can do that many scripts a day at a time when I'm filming, I'm 100% certain you can make time to write your scripts.

Now, I want you to pause here and write at least one script right now. Use this formula:

- Research viral videos
- Save viral ideas in your Notes app on your phone
- Study the viral videos you saved and steal the hook, the subject matter, or the delivery
- Write your own scripts based off the Hook-Personality-Value-CTA formula

Now, let's move on to recording.

Batch Recording

This section contains advice for beginners as well as coaches who are already making $10,000 or more a month.

If you're a beginner, here's your complete guide to filming high-value content. You'll need:

- A ring light
- A phone you can record video with

Any ring light from Amazon will do. The most important part of filming by yourself to get yourself in an energetic and excited mood before you film. If you come across boring, no one will want to listen to your videos.

We all have a regular voice and a camera voice. In my opinion, your camera voice needs to be more pronounced and energetic then your regular conversation voice. Do whatever you have to do to get yourself in a good mood before you film. You could call a friend first, scream at the top of your lungs, or dance to your favorite song.

When you record, follow these rules and you'll absolutely smash it:

1. Have your camera positioned at eye level. It shouldn't be above or below you. This will make your videos more natural —like you're talking directly to someone.

2. If your whole body (head to toes) is in the video, try to have your head at 75%. You don't want your head at the top of the Instagram Reel frame—it'll get cut off in the newsfeed. You also don't want your head in the middle of the video because it looks weird.

3. To look good on camera, lighting needs to be in front of you. That's why I recommend a ring light. If you have a ring light, you can set up the light in front of you, which makes filming easier. If you don't have a ring light, film in front of a window, so the light from outside is in front of you. This will provide good lighting, which is essential if you want to grow on social media.

4. Film one line at a time. Memorize your line, press record, read the next line, and end the recording. Continue this until you've read your entire script. I used to try to memorize my entire script and record it all in one go, but I'd get extremely frustrated if I messed up a line and had to start again. Pro tip: Before you end your recording, pause for a moment and keep looking at the camera. When you cut the video in post-edit, you want to make sure that you're not looking away at the end of your sentence.
5. Change the scene behind you every 1.5 to 3 seconds. This is the single most important aspect of filming content that goes viral. Move rooms, change locations, do whatever you need to do to keep changing your surroundings. Your video cannot be boring, and the way you make it interesting is to keep changing the scene.
6. Next thing I want you to do is change the directions you face, so you aren't always looking directly at the camera. Start with the ring light facing you and you're facing the camera. Deliver your line and end your recording. Then, move your ring light to your right side. Remain standing forward toward your camera, but film the next line looking over to your right at the ring light. After you deliver that line, move the ring light to your left side. Remain standing forward toward the camera, but when you record and deliver your line, you're going to look to your left at the ring light.

You can also do this in post-edit. Remember that something needs to change in the video every 1.5–3 seconds. So, you could use a slow zoom, a jump cut, add a graphic to the video, or use a sound effect. Do something every few seconds that keeps your viewers' attention on the video.

Here are a few examples:

> For recipe videos, show yourself making the recipe, use b-roll shots, and add a voiceover.

For business-related videos that involve numbers, use a whiteboard to draw out your visuals.

For sales-related videos, record a role-play sales call and have someone give you an objection and you overcome it.

For content coaches, do a screen-recording of the opening three seconds of one of your client's viral videos and break down exactly what you did to help them go viral.

For talking videos, you could deliver the same value by using props as you speak. For instance, if you're fitness coach you could buy one pound of fat and one pound of muscle props online and use them as visuals in your videos. If you're a real estate agent, you could use a "sold" sign as a prop in your content.

There are so many ways to approach filming that will make your content more engaging, but for now, these five rules will get you massive traction.

Guide to Filming if You Make $10,000 or More a Month

The best investment you can make is back into your business. If you're making more than $10,000 a month you must understand that the primary vehicle that drives your business is content creation, so producing high-value content on a consistent schedule is important. I recommend finding a videographer to record your content for you.

How much does that service cost? You'll likely be able to find someone to film fourteen Reels for you, including color grading and cutting out empty spaces between lines for $500 to $1,000 per shoot. I wouldn't pay much more than that when first getting started. The most I'd be willing to pay is $1,000 for fourteen very well-done Reels. You can negotiate with videographers as well for $500 to $1,000 for completed Reels with captions included.

Personally, I invest more than $21,000 a month for my media team, which is why I'm able to produce high quality content at a consistent volume. If you're making $10,000 or more a month, reinvest some of that money back into your business so you can make *more* money.

You may have to coach your videographer to produce exactly what you need. Unfortunately, not many videographers understand how to go viral on social media, so, I coached my videographer on exactly how I wanted my video content shot. I also recommend building a long-term relationship with your videographer. Use that information during your pricing negotiations.

To find a videographer in your city, start by asking your social media network if anyone knows of any videographers in the area who might be interested in shooting content with you. You can also search local Facebook groups in your area. If you wanted to take it a step further, you could create a job posting on Indeed. You can also search your city or area code with "photographer" as a hashtag on Instagram. For example, #yycphotographer. There are tons of photographers out there, you just have to properly search for them.

If you're going to shoot with a videographer, my best advice is to start with two shoots a month and get content for fourteen Reels at a time. If you are more advanced and have extra capital, then I recommend shooting once a week and getting content for seven to fourteen each week.

I film with my videographer twice a week and we get content for twenty to thirty Reels every shoot.

If you work with a videographer, set clear expectations from the onset of the working relationship. Here's what I mean by that. When I record content with my videographer, I expect to receive content that is ready to post or edit in my email inbox within 48 hours after the shoot.

If the videographer is editing all your Reels, the 48-hour wait time means you're receiving all your edited Reels that are ready to post within 48 hours after the shoot. If your videographer is color grading the Reels, and you're handling the edits yourself or sending them to a video editor, then I'd expect your videos back within 24 hours. Set these expectations from the beginning, so you don't film and then have to wait a week to get your content.

A Guide to Batch Recording Your Content Based on Your Level

Beginner Filming Self: 60–120 Minutes per week (seven Reels at a time)

Beginner Filming with Videographer: 60–120 Minutes every two weeks (fourteen Reels at a time)

Advanced Filming with Videographer: 60–120 Minutes per week (seven to fourteen Reels per shoot)

How to Batch Edit Your Content

Editing your Reels isn't that hard, especially with the tools we have now. I'm going to cover how to edit your content as a beginner, as well as how to edit your content if you have more advanced skills or you're making more than $10,000 a month and can afford to invest in a video editor.

If you're a complete beginner, edit your content using Submagic.io. It's $20 to $40 a month and the program uses AI to edit your videos for you—it's awesome. When you use Submagic.co keep these rules in mind:

1. Choose a simple font. As a complete beginner you don't need to worry about being fancy, just focus on keeping the process simple and easy, so you can maintain consistency. That means choosing a simple, clean font.
2. Don't use b-roll stock or your own videos. No one wants to watch a video of some random person on a phone at their desk.

3. Make sure you cut out all the dead space in your video. I almost want your sentences to run into one another.

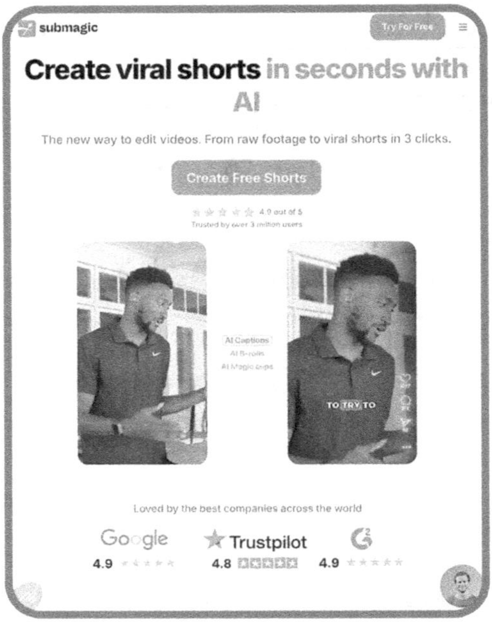

Submagic.co has a tool that allows you to remove bad takes, which should eliminate all the dead space in your videos. If it doesn't, you can do it yourself by tapping the bar at the bottom of the video and trimming the video. Once you trim the video, and your sentences are clean and smoothly run into each other with no dead space, then you're going to add captions to the video.

Keep the captions as short as possible. You should also add "hook title" on your video during the opening three seconds of your videos. A hook-title is similar to the hook you use in the video; it should describe what your video is about and why they should pay attention. If you scroll over to "boost," you'll see "AI hook title."

You can use the hook title they give you or you can use the idea to create a scroll stopping hook that we've talked about.

When you batch edit all your videos at the same time, you'll have content you can post for an entire week.

CHAPTER 6

How to Batch Edit Your Content if You Make $10,000+ a Month

You can pay with time or you pay with money. Rich people spend money to save time. So, if you have extra capital you're going to hire a video editor. If you have a large social media following (10,000 or more people), you may be able to find one by posting on your social media that you're hiring video editors. If you don't have a large social media following, however, you're going to have to get creative. There are two places you can go to find video editors. They are: Fivers and Upwork.

Both websites list freelancers who are currently looking for work. To start, you're going to sort through the profiles that offer Reels editing for $15 to $30 per Reel. I want you to hire five people. You're going to give the exact same raw footage to all five of them. You're also going to send all of them the same example of what you want your content to look like. When you're first getting started, it's best to keep it simple. You can even send them some of my content if you want.

Inform the videographers that you've hired five people for the same project to see what everyone comes up with and your goal is to hire someone to be your full-time videographer. Let the videographers know you hire based off two things. The first is the quality of the Reel you get back. The second is the speed in which they return their completed work. You're going to hire someone to do seven to fourteen Reels a week, so you need someone who can do a great job in a short timeframe.

Here's an email script you can copy to send to your five potential video editors.

Email Script Sample

> Hey [name] I'm hiring you for a specific test project.
>
> I'm looking to hire a full-time editor to do seven to fourteen Instagram Reels a week for me. I am hiring four other video editors, like yourself, to

> do the exact same job. I've attached the sample footage I'd like you to make my video look like, and your goal is to create an Instagram Reel that is engaging, simple, and easy to watch.
>
> I also want you to change the scene every 1.5 to 3 seconds by adding a jump cut, slow zoom, or any other effect to make the video engaging.
>
> I don't want any b-roll in the video. I also want you to make sure you cut out any dead space between my sentences.
>
> I will be selecting a video editor based off the quality of your work and the speed in which you get it back to me.
>
> Thank you for your time!
> [Name]

Once you find your video editor, you'll have someone who will do videos for $15 to $30 per Reel, which means you'll spend $420 to $840 a month on video edits. But that frees up a lot of your time to focus on income generating activities.

If you sign just *one* client because you freed up ten to thirty hours, the return on investment (ROI) is not only worth it, but it doubles. That's how you're going to scale.

The same rule applies to hiring editors as it does to hiring videographers. Before you officially hire an editor, you need to make it clear that when you get them a batch of seven to fourteen Reels that you expect those fully edited, high-quality Reels in your inbox within 48 hours. Seventy-two hours is the absolute max. That way, you don't have to wait forever to get your content.

CHAPTER 6

SUMMARY

In this chapter we discussed how to batch write your scripts. I gave you a step-by-step formula for how to find viral ideas, as well as content scripts you can steal and start using for your business.

Then we talked about how to record your content as a beginner and how to record if you're a more advanced individual who has capital to invest in your content.

Finally, we talked about how to batch edit your content, so you can get it all done in one go. That way, you're ready for the social media takeover.

And with that, now you know how to batch content like a $10,000,000 coach.

CHAPTER 7

THE $10,000,000 INSTAGRAM CONTENT SCHEDULE

While I wrote this book, I posted six times a day on Instagram, seven days a week. I don't recommend that posting schedule if you're just getting started. So, what *is* the best content schedule for you? The answer is simple: The best posting schedule is the one you can stick to.

My definition of consistency is once a day, every day, seven days a week. For me, that is the bare minimum. However, you might not be able to commit to that posting schedule right now. You might have a full-time job, kids, or other responsibilities you're committed to. That being said, what you first need to do is you need to identify the number of posts you can realistically commit to posting on social media and commit to that posting schedule.

Never miss.

Don't make a commitment you can't keep, and don't break a commitment you've made. Now, we're going to identify how much time you realistically have to commit to create content every week. Then, we'll create a schedule based off the time you can commit.

Let's break it down.

If you have thirty minutes to two hours a day that you can realistically commit to creating content, that's cool. If you have two to four hours to create content, also cool. All things considered, with kids, your health goals, your client work, your relationship, time with friends and family, how much time do you realistically have to commit to your content creation for Instagram?

Decide on a number now.

Choose a timeframe anywhere between thirty minutes and four hours a day. Once you have your realistic time you can commit to every day, you'll have to break down your week based on the theory we've talked about in the previous chapter.

- How much time are you going to spend ideating?
- How much time scripting?
- How much time recording?
- How much time editing videos?

Plan out your week based off the time you committed to, and the amount of time you post on social media is going to be 100% predicated on the amount of time you can realistically commit to.

Here are three posting schedules based on three business phases: Part-Time Coach, Full-Time Coach, and Growth-Mode Coach.

Part-Time Coach (30 min–1 hour/day)

If you're starting your online business as a side hustle, but it's still important to you, this is your posting schedule. You're going to post three to five times a week and you're going to post on Facebook and Instagram. Your posts are going to be a combination of connection, proof and value content. They'll be delivered as either awareness content, meaning content designed for a wider audience, or conversion content, meaning content designed specifically to speak to your ideal client avatar.

Three to five times a day you're going to post on your Instagram Stories. (More on exactly how to use Instagram Stories to attract clients in the coming chapters). You will document your day and take your audience on an adventure and show them behind the scenes of you living the lifestyle.

As a part-time coach, you're going to publish two call-to-action (CTA) posts per week. A CTA is where you post directly or indirectly for clients to reach out about your coaching offer (more on this in the coming chapter).

You're also going to do one Instagram Livestream per week. For your livestream, you can go live and talk about a subject you did a post about or you the livestream can be longer and more drawn out with a longer explanation as you give value to your audience.

Example of a Part-Time Online Coach Posting Schedule

Your Newsfeed

Monday: The biggest mistake in your ideal [client journey].

Tuesday: My client, [name], got [X] result in [X timeframe].

Wednesday: Never, ever, ever do [this] on your journey.

Thursday: Stop thinking [this wrong thing] is the solution to your problem.

Friday: Steal my cheat sheet to get [Specific Result].

Instagram Stories

Post three to five Stories documenting your day (one to two should be social proof slides)

CTA Schedule

Once on Monday: Facebook, Instagram Stories, and Instagram Newsfeed

Once on Thursday: Facebook and Instagram Stories

Livestream Schedule

Wednesday: Go live and talk in more detail about a post you published

Full-Time Coach Phase (1–2 hours/day)

If you're a full-time online coach and you're ready to take your business to the next level, then I'm going to give you the ideal content schedule for your business. You're going to post seven times a week and you're going to post on Facebook and Instagram. Posts are going to be a combination of connection, proof, and value content. They'll be delivered as either awareness content, meaning content designed for a wider audience, or conversion content, meaning content designed specifically to speak to your ideal client avatar.

Five to seven times a day, you're going to post on Instagram Stories. You will document your day and take your audience on an adventure and show them behind the scenes of you living the lifestyle.

As a full-time coach, you're going to publish two call-to-action (CTA) posts per week. A CTA is where you post directly or indirectly for clients to reach out about your coaching offer.

You're also going to do two to three Instagram Livestreams per week. For your livestream, you can go live and talk about a subject you did a post about or you the livestream can be longer and more drawn out with a longer explanation as you give value to your audience.

Example of a Full-Time Online Coach Posting Schedule

Your Newsfeed

- Monday: The biggest mistake you're making on [your journey].
- Tuesday: My client, [name], got [X] result in [X timeframe].
- Wednesday: Never, ever, ever do [this] on your journey.
- Thursday: Stop thinking [this wrong thing] is the solution to your problem.
- Friday: Steal my cheat sheet to get [specific result].
- Saturday: Day in the Life of an Online Coach who [Does X].
- Sunday: You're ruining your [weekday] progress on the weekends.

Instagram Stories

Post five to seven Stories documenting your day (two to three should be social proof slides)

CTA Schedule

Once on Monday: Facebook, Instagram Stories, and Instagram Newsfeed

Once on Thursday: Facebook and Instagram Stories

LIVESTREAM SCHEDULE:

Monday: Go live and talk in more detail about a post you published

Friday: Go live and do a Q+A session

Growth-Mode Online Coach (2–4 hours/day)

If you're in growth mode and ready to take your business to new heights and you have the time to *fully* commit to your content creation process and online business, this is the ideal schedule for you. You're going to post twice a day every day of the week, and you're going to post on Facebook and Instagram. Posts are going to be a combination of connection, proof, and value content. They'll be delivered as either awareness content, meaning content designed for a wider audience, or conversion content, meaning content designed specifically to speak to your ideal client avatar.

Five to seven times a day, you're going to post on Instagram Stories. You will document your day and take your audience on an adventure and show them behind the scenes of you living the lifestyle.

As a growth-mode coach, you're going to publish three call-to-action (CTA) posts per week. A CTA is where you post directly or indirectly for clients to reach out about your coaching offer.

You're also going to do three to five Instagram Livestreams per week. For your livestream, you can go live and talk about a subject you did a post about or you the livestream can be longer and more drawn out with a longer explanation as you give value to your audience.

Example of a Growth-Mode Online Coaching Posting Schedule

Your Newsfeed

> Monday: Post 1—The biggest mistake you're making on [your journey]. / Post 2—Relatable awareness Reel
>
> Tuesday: Post —My client, [name], got [X] result in [X timeframe]. / Post 2—Stop making [this mistake].

Wednesday: Post 1—Never, ever, ever do [this] on your journey. / Post 2—Relatable awareness Reel

Thursday: Post 1—Stop making [this mistake] on your journey. Post 2—Steal this secret that [got specific result].

Friday: Post 1—Steal my cheat sheet to get [specific result]. / Post 2—My client, [name], got [X] result.

Saturday: Post 1—Day in the Life of an Online Coach who [Does X]. / Post 2—Relatable weekend Reel

Sunday: 1—You're Ruining Your [weekday] progress on the weekends. / Post 2—Goal-setting Sunday Reel

Instagram Stories

Post five to seven Stories documenting your day (two to three should be social proof slides)

CTA Schedule

(You can post more CTAs when you post more value.)

Once on Monday: Facebook, Instagram Stories, and Instagram Newsfeed

Once on Wednesday: Facebook, Instagram Stories, and Instagram Newsfeed

Once on Thursday: Facebook, Instagram Stories, and Instagram Newsfeed

Livestream Schedule

Monday: Go live and talk in more detail about a post you published

Wednesday: Go live and do a Q+A session

Friday: Go live and talk with a client

SUMMARY

Your goal with content creation is to find a schedule you can stick to. Don't commit to a schedule you can't stick to. And, once you commit—stick to it. That's why you need to be realistic about the amount of time you can commit to creating your content. For most online coaches, you are better off starting with the part-time online coach phase and get yourself in the flow. You'll start to feel good about your posting schedule.

Once you become consistent, and content creation is easier for you, then slowly increase your posting volume. When your views pick up (because you are studying your content and figuring out how you can make it better), then you can increase your posting volume. Start with consistency, then move to quality, and finish with volume.

See you in the next chapter! I'm going to show you *exactly* how to turn warm prospects in your audience into leads in your inbox.

Let's *go*!

CHAPTER 8

CLIENT ACQUISITION STRATEGIES

I book six hundred sales calls a month. Out of those six hundred sales calls a month, three hundred of them come from Instagram. On top of those three hundred sales calls that I generate from Instagram, I also generate three hundred sales by chat opportunities, where a prospect has lower amounts of funds. Instead of booking a call with them, I send them program details over Instagram DMs. I started from zero.

In 2018, I decided that I no longer wanted to be an online fitness coach and instead, I wanted to be *the* business coach for online fitness coaches. At the time, I built my own successful online fitness business to $50,000 a month. To be honest, I was no longer passionate about online fitness coaching. Throughout my time running Aesthetic Nation, my fitness business, I hired and mentored trainers to work underneath my brand. I was responsible for helping them build their businesses.

There was a massive problem though. Fifty percent of the time, there was an issue. Sometimes it was personal other times it was financial, but eventually it caused us to part ways. So, I basically trained people to become my competition, and I didn't get paid for it.

Up until I decided to shift my business focus, I posted content like "How to lose weight" for five years. Imagine my audience's shock when I changed my content to how much money I made off them. It wasn't good!

In 2018, I was fighting to find leads because I started from zero. I had a few people who watched me build my online fitness business. They were in my circle and were immediately interested. Beyond that, however, getting clients proved to be a challenge. I tried everything. I was in Facebook groups adding random friends. I was on Instagram following random personal trainers from hashtags. I even created a LinkedIn account to send one hundred reach outs a day.

While the strategy of shooting my shot one thousand times a day proved to be effective to get my first few clients, it sure as hell wasn't effective to grow my business beyond the $30,000 a month mark.

When I hired Taki Moore, everything changed. He is the goat of the goats. I'd say 90% of the internet marketers that you look up to have been through Taki Moore's program. When I found Taki, I was making up to $30,000 a month with my business consulting company, and up to $30,000 a month with my online fitness business. When I reached out to Taki, I told him, "I want to make one hundred thousand dollars a month by the time I turn twenty-eight years old." That birthday happened to be seven months away.

Taki said that wouldn't be a problem at all. I needed that reassurance, so I hired him.

I spent $25,000 over the next year, and the information I learned in Taki's program completely changed my life. His program is where I learned a fundamental understanding of the client acquisition strategies I'm going to talk about with you in this chapter.

I knew enough to make me money before Taki. After Taki—I was a weapon, baby.

I took the fundamentals Taki passed along to me and I've created a blueprint you can use to consistently sign clients across your social media platforms.

CHAPTER 8

In this chapter, I am not going to gatekeep. Instead, I'm giving you *all* the client acquisition strategies I use to book three hundred sales calls a month, three hundred sell-by-chat opportunities a month, and all the secrets revealed behind my ten million dollar a year coaching empire.

Before we can talk acquisition, we need to talk about the value that you're providing on social media. The amount of money you make on social media is directly related to the amount of value that you give on social media. And remember, my definition of value is that your content is so good that people can get results without hiring you. Without this as a fundamental baseline, your social media efforts to sign clients will be in vain. You *must* make the commitment that you are going to be the most valuable person for your ideal client on Instagram. That must be where this comes from.

I want you to imagine your social media as a bank account. If you walked into a bank, that you've never made a deposit into and you asked, "Can I make a withdrawal?" The teller would look at you confused, say you don't have an account, and send you on your way. If you persisted in asking for withdrawal, they'd call security, escort your ass out, and that would be the end. Unfortunately, that's how most of you approach social media. You post basic, generic content that doesn't give any value.

And then you go to your audience, and you try to make a withdrawal. "Hey, you guys want to buy from me?" Your audience looks at your content, looks at your ask, and thinks "why would I buy from you? I don't get any value from you." So, you think, "Oh, they're ghosting me, I just have follow up with them." Maybe the reason they're ghosting you is they don't want to work with you because you haven't deposited any value for them.

The Law of Reciprocity

The law of reciprocity states that people feel significantly more inclined to want to give back to you when they have already received something from you. That's why, if you work in sales, you offer someone coffee or water when they walk into your office. Providing a "gift" is a very good move for you. It's also why, if you're on social media you need to make the commitment that you are going to give so much damn value that you literally blow people's minds with how much you give away. That is how you prime your social media to make money.

Your CTA schedule should always be three to one, which means you give three pieces of information for every one ask you make. This follows the Gary Vee rule of "Jab, Jab, Jab, Right Hook."

Client Acquisition Strategies

1. Hard Call to Actions
2. Soft Call to Actions
3. Instagram Livestreams to Podcasts
4. Fourteen-Day Challenges
5. Flash Sales
6. Magnetic Giveaways
7. Other Ways to Get Clients (Story Sequences)

A fundamental principle that you need to remember across all these lead generation strategies is urgency and scarcity, which create the fear of missing out, or FOMO. You know that feeling when you were in high school and you couldn't go to a party because you had to study? You hated that you missed out on the party! That's FOMO. It's one of the most powerful ways to encourage people to act now and not later. You can cause FOMO just by the way you position your marketing.

The smartest brands use FOMO to get you to buy right now. When you buy airline tickets from a website or book a hotel, you're going to see FOMO, urgency, and scarcity messaging sprinkled over the website. Phrases like "only two seats left at this price," will push you to purchase your plane ticket right away or the price will go up. Do we ever know if there are *truly* only two seats left at that rate? No.

I do know that people are predictable, and you can use that to your advantage when you market your services. There are a lot of conflicting opinions on this because it's tinkering on the dark side of persuasion, but here's my argument. You're not selling vacuum cleaners. You're selling an online coaching service that genuinely helps people change their lives for the better. Your ideal client is better off in your program, than in your competitor's program because you are going to go above and beyond and *actually* serve them. I know that, because you wouldn't be reading my book if you didn't care about growing your business, helping people, and learning how to do so. So, you need to use urgency and scarcity in your marketing, and I'm going to show you different ways to do exactly that. Understand, however, that without urgency and scarcity there's no reason for people to want to take action now, which means your business won't grow. You need to give people a reason to act. If they don't, they might miss out.

1. Hard CTA

A hard CTA is when you directly ask your audience if they'd like to join your coaching program. Typically speaking, you want to be more direct and straight to the point with this type of CTA. Call out the specific avatar or the specific pain point your target audience would like to solve.

In your hard CTA, you are going to use urgency and scarcity to encourage people to act now. In terms of the best time to post hard CTAs, my advice is to always post them on Mondays. It doesn't matter what industry you are in; Monday is the day to take a new action. It's the day people get off the weekend vibe and they go to work, which means they're already in the mode of taking action. Monday is also the day when people get back on track. It's is also day of the week when people go to jobs they may not like. So, posting a CTA to change their life on a Monday is always going to be powerful.

Hard CTAs on Instagram Stories

Before you post a CTA on Instagram Stories, you're going to delete all the active Stories you have up. That way, your CTA post is your only active Instagram Story. Don't post anything else for at least twelve hours after you post your CTA. Doing so actually hacks the Instagram algorithm.

When you only have one story up, and it's your CTA, your audience can engage with it. This signals to Instagram that people want to see your Story, so it pushes out that piece of content to a wider audience. As a result, more people see, vote, and interact with your CTA Story post.

When you post a CTA on your Instagram stories, always use a photo when you use the hack.

Why? Photo's work better. But there are only a few different types of photos I recommend. They are:

1. Before and after photos (of yourself or your clients)

2. High quality professional photo of you

3. Screenshot of a client win

Take one of the three photo elements and post it to your Instagram Stories and then write on the photo.

Here are five CTAs you can use on your Instagram Story to attract clients:

1. I'm looking for five [ideal clients] who want [specific result] in [specific time frame]. If that's you, vote below.
2. Do you want to get [specific result] in [specific time frame]? I have two spots remaining to [get rid of pain point]. If you want in, vote here.
3. I'm starting a brand new case study program for [X] person tomorrow. So, if you want to get [this result], have [this character trait], and are friendly and coachable, vote below.
4. I will help you get [specific result] in specific [time frame] or you don't pay. Want in? Vote here.
5. I helped my client [name], get specific [result] in specific [time frame]. Want results like this? Vote here.

If you take one of those CTAs and can post it with a before and after photo, it'll look like this:

If you take another CTA and post it with a high-quality professional photo, your Instagram Story would look like this:

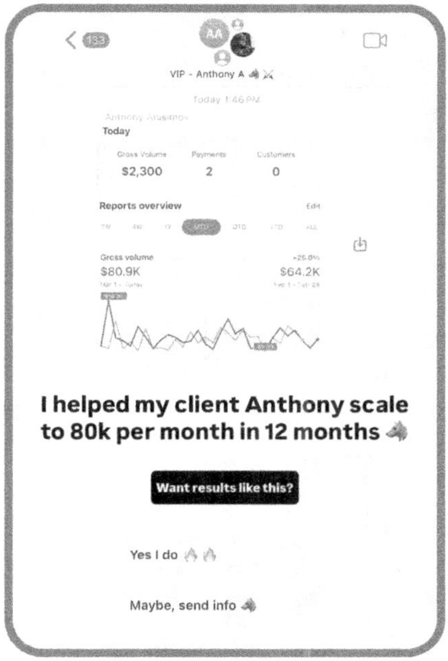

If you use CTA and can post it with a screenshot of a client win, it'll look like this:

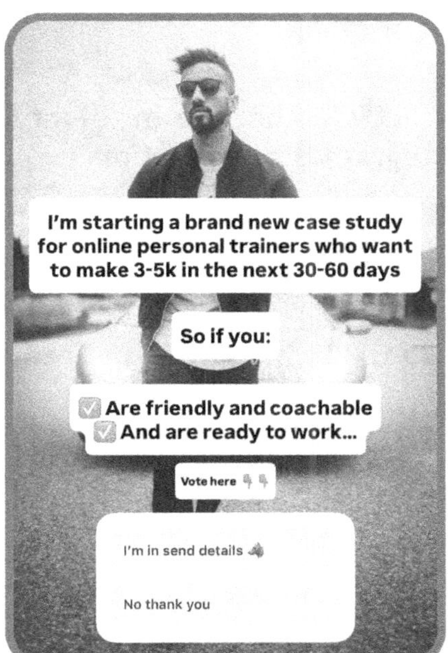

In seconds, I took the exact same CTA and I gave it a different feel. Now that you know this information, you can use the five CTAs I've given you and you can run each one of them three ways, which means you have fifteen CTAs from this one idea.

Great marketing is about saying the same thing one hundred ways. You're selling the same program, you're wrapping it up and delivering it in different languages.

If you're in the fat-loss niche, some people will resonate more with the word "toned" than they will with the phrase "lose weight." That means, when you use the word "toned" as part of your CTA, you'll get a higher response rate.

A great marketer understands this. So, you need to find one hundred ways to say the same thing so you grab people's attention. Your audience has a specific result they want to accomplish and once you name that specific result with the right word or phrase, they'll reach out.

Hard CTAs in Your Newsfeed

On your Newsfeed, meaning you post a Carousel or an Instagram Reel, you're going to use the exact same five CTAs we discussed above. For your in-feed posts, however, you can get creative and tell a bit of a story.

There are two type of CTAs you can use in your Newsfeed posts:

1. Short, direct CTAs that use any of the language included in the Instagram Stories section
2. Longer, direct CTAs that use a story of your success or a client's success and what you did to get results.

Short, Direct Hard CTAs in Your Newsfeed

A short, direct, hard CTA would be a before and after photo of a client with text that reads, "I'm looking for five [ideal clients] who want [specific result] in [specific time frame]. If that's you, vote below."

Another example would be a six-second, b-roll video with text on screen that reads, "I naturally lost one hundred pounds in twelve months without giving up my favorite foods. If you want to learn how I did it, comment TONED and I'll show you."

Finally, a third example would be an Instagram Carousel post with the text "I'm starting a brand new case study program for [X] person tomorrow. So, if you want to get [this result, have [this character trait], and are friendly and coachable."

In simple terms, cut straight to the point and tell your audience your exact offer. This works well if you've developed goodwill with your audience and people watch your content and get value from it. When you do these types of CTAs, the more drastic the transformation you can find, the better. I used to only post realistic transformations and I wouldn't post my best clients because I wanted it to be attainable for everyone. Don't, do that. It's stupid.

If you have clients in your program who are absolutely smashing it, use those clients in your CTAs, so your audience can see what results look like when they decide to reach out and follow your advice.

Longer, Direct CTAs in Your Newsfeed

If you post a longer CTA, and you want to do a written post as a before and after, I got you. Follow this template:

If you want to post a longer, direct, CTA as an Instagram Reel, use your storytelling skills. This type of content has become one of my favorite ways to do social proof because it gives value at the same time. You'll tell a story of how you helped a client get a specific result and you'll give away a bit of the secret sauce regarding exactly how you did it.

You tell them what you did, you don't tell them how you did it.

The format is simple.

You can use CTA text like these examples:

> My client [name], got [X] result in [X] time frame, and in this video I'm going to teach you exactly how we did it.
>
> When [name] first reached out he was struggling with [this thing, this thing, and this thing]. So, the first change we decided to make was [specific thing].
>
> We also did [this thing and this thing] and after implementing just these three things my client reached out and said he was feeling [this type of way] and he was so stoked with the results that he me [insert a testimonial photo or video here].
>
> If you want my help setting this up for you, comment [keyword] and I'll reach out to you to see if I can help."

You can see my highly edited version of this, but I also have some variations I can show you.

You can deliver the information by using a whiteboard. You can deliver the information by telling a story. You can even deliver the information by holding your phone and then showing the client results on your computer screen.

Tell a story, give some value, and then do a hard CTA at the end of the video.

You must put your hard CTA as the first line in your caption. The only exception to this is when you're doing a social proof written post template. Why? Because it's the only thing people see when they scroll through Reels and land on your content. They have to tap three little buttons if they want to read the full caption.

2. Soft CTAs

A soft CTA is when you indirectly ask clients to work with you. Oftentimes, you'll use what the marketing world refers to as a lead magnet. It's a honeypot for the ideal client that you'd like to target to engage with. When you use a traditional lead magnet, it would be a free eBook or resource because of interacting with you. While that's one way of doing a soft CTA, is not the only way.

To effectively do a "soft CTA, which is calling your ideal clients to act in some way like voting on a poll, engaging on a Story, or commenting on a post you have to think about something that's related to their journey and then put out the honey pot. Soft CTAs are an effective way to get more people to reach out, but the intent to purchase tends to be a little bit lower.

Think about the psychology of someone who directly responds to a post that reads, "I'm looking for five men who want to lose ten pounds in thirty days." That man is in the psychology of wanting to take action to lose weight now. On the other hand, think about the psychology of someone who votes on a post that reads, "If you lost five pounds a month, how many months would it take to get to your goal weight?" Someone who votes may be scrolling through Instagram and votes for the sake of voting.

That being said, these CTAs are still an effective strategy to get people to raise their hands. Whether they're interested in purchasing your product or service now or not, the fact of the matter is that they engaged with your post. They could have scrolled. They could have swiped away. Instead they engaged, which means we get a peek into their mind.

They wouldn't engage on your post if, on some level, they didn't struggle with the specific information you shared. Someone struggling with an issue that you can solve is half the battle when selling your online coaching program.

So, a soft CTA is offered with the intention of getting your prospects to engage with your Instagram Stories. When they interact, they show they have a problem that you can solve. You can then use that information to start a conversation.

Soft CTAs on Instagram Stories

In this section, you'll find a long list of poll ideas that are separated based on industry. You can use these polls in your Instagram Stories for soft-sell CTAs that will engage your audience. If your industry isn't listed, take a picture of this page on your phone and upload it to ChatGPT. Add this prompt: Please give me a list of fifty questions I can ask my audience like this for my avatar. My avatar is [X] person and wants to get [X] goal.

Soft Call to Actions on Your Instagram Newsfeed

You can do shorter CTAs that advertise a lead magnet or free resource you've created for your ideal client or you can post longer videos that give value and then give *more* value at the end of the video by getting the audience to comment a keyword to receive more value. Both are effective. When you post soft CTAs to your newsfeed make sure it's something that's tangible that people can grip onto. You have to give them a specific reason to *want* to leave a comment. That specific reason is that they will get something tangible that they can use to get results.

If your soft CTA doesn't get engagement it means that either your content sucks, your lead magnet wasn't valuable enough, your lead magnet wasn't positioned well enough to get people to comment with a keyword for more value.

I personally post videos where I'll say, "The worst way to post on your Instagram Stories is [X]." At the end of the video I'll say, "If you want my full guide to selling on Instagram Stories, comment the word GUIDE, and I'll send it over."

I've also used, "Steal this ChatGPT prompt to come up with viral content ideas." I add a specific ChatGPT prompt to the video. Then I finish the video by saying, "Comment the word PROMPT, and I'll send it over."

Fitness Coach

If you're a fitness coach, you could post a glute workout video that gave you a crazy transformation. At the end of the video say, "Comment the word BOOTY, and I'll send you my full routine."

Sales Coach

If you're a sales coach, you could give away a talking track that help people close when they get a prospect who says, "I need to think about it." At the end of the video you say, "Comment the word SCRIPT, and I'll send you the exact talking track you need to close prospects when they say this."

Relationship Coach

If you're a relationship coach, talk about how you and your partner have date night every week and how on date night you always sit down and have hard conversations if they need to be had. At the end of the video, you can say "Comment DATE NIGHT, and I'll send you the framework for how to have hard conversations with the person you love."

Content Coach

If you're a content coach, you could give your audience the posting schedule they need to attract clients on a regular basis. Then at the end of the video you could say, "If you want the full schedule, including post examples, comment CONTENT, and I'll send it over."

The value must be tangible enough for them to grip on to.

Manychat

Go to Manychat.com. Create an account and connect your Instagram to Manychat. After you do that, publish your CTA post. Then, go into Manychat and set up an automated message that directly sends a resource when someone comments a specific word on that CTA post. Using Manychat will save you time because you won't have to manually send a resource to every person who leaves a comment on your post or replies to a Story.

Here's how to create a Manychat automation:

1. Tap "Automations"

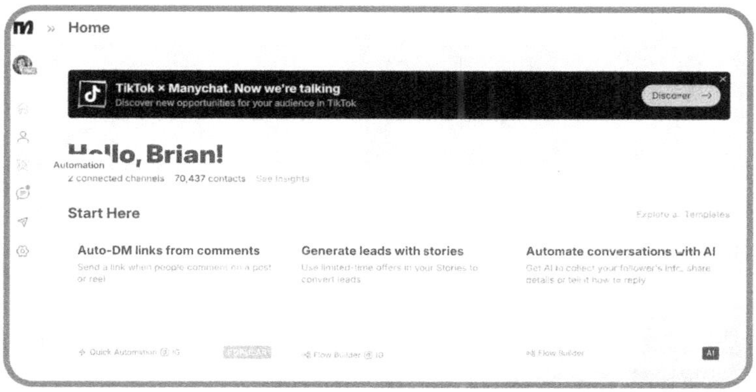

2. Tap "New Automation"

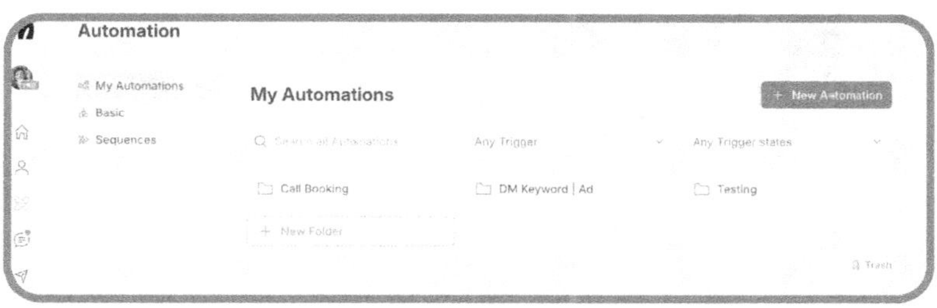

3. Tap "Start from Scratch"

4. Tap “New Trigger”

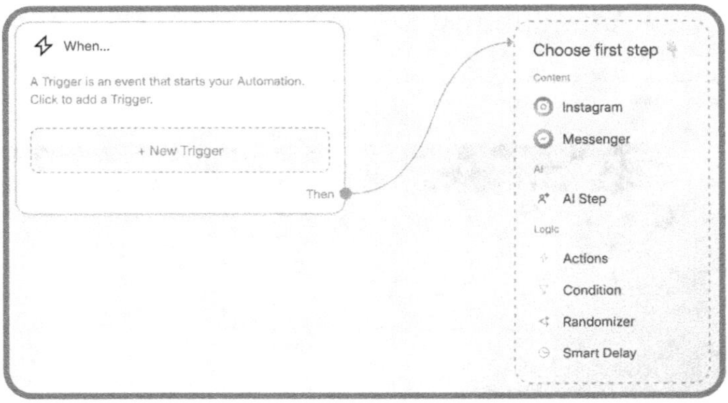

5. Tap “User comments on post or Reel”

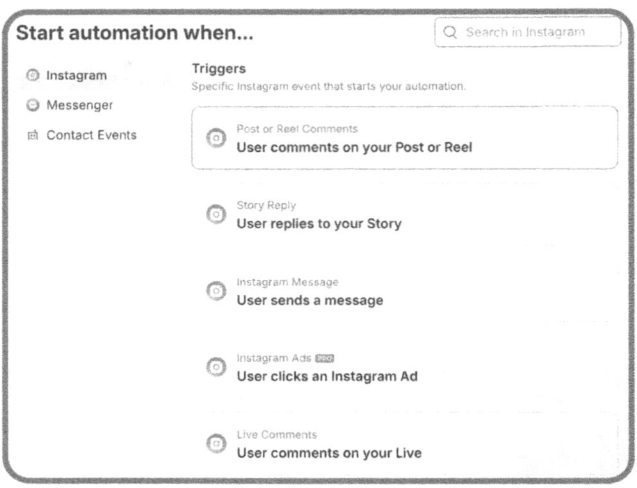

6. Tap the specific post/Reel that you'd like to attach the Manychat to

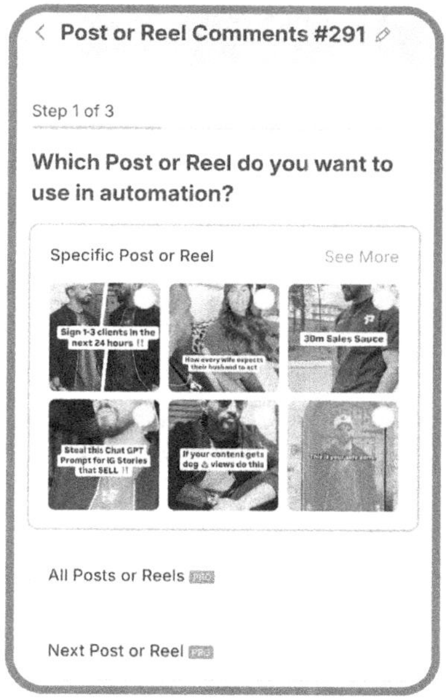

7. Type in the keyword you said in your photo or Reel.

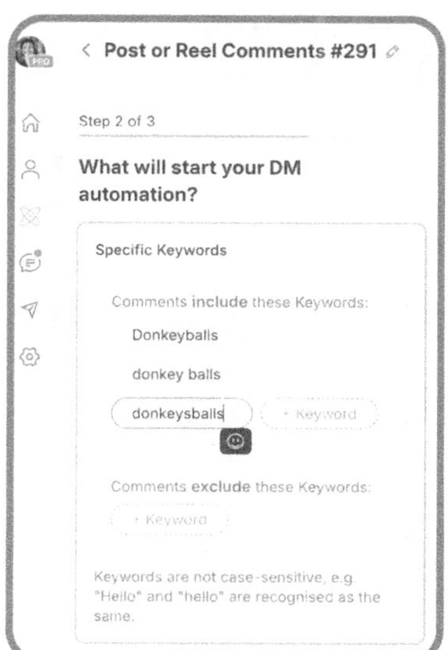

8. Type in three to four different ways to spell your keyword because sometimes your audience messes up the spelling
9. Turn off auto replies to the comment (This has restricted my account before, and it's not worth it to auto comment reply.)

10. Press "Save"
11. That's going to send an Instagram message.
12. Tap "Add text"

13. Add text that says something like: "Hey! Here's [X resource] you asked for. P.S. I'm looking for five men who want to lose ten pounds in the next thirty days. If you're interested reply BURN, and I'll reach out to see if I can help."

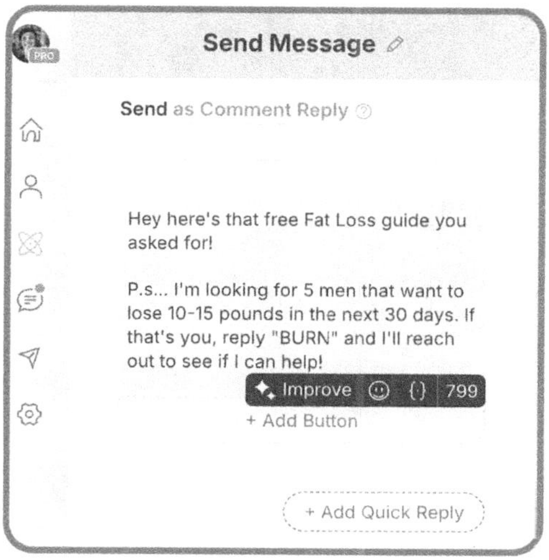

14. Once you add the text, tap "Add button"
15. You can name the button "Fat loss guide"

16. Then LINK the button to a specific link. (I recommend uploading any PDF or free resource to Dropbox that you want to send out.)

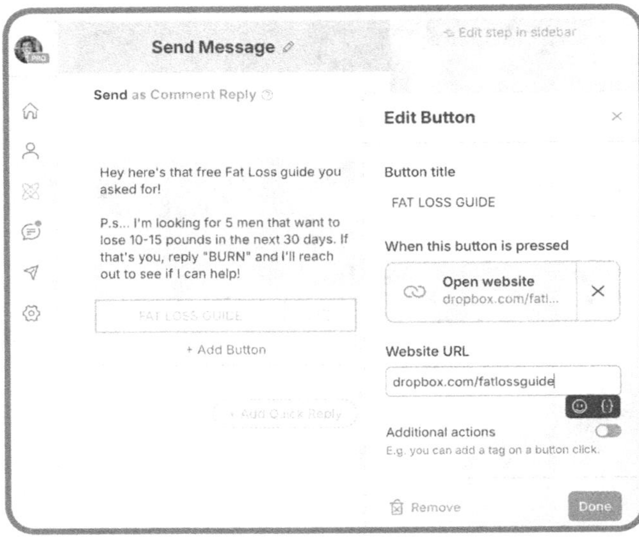

17. Tap "Open website"
18. Paste the link to your free resource in the "open website" button

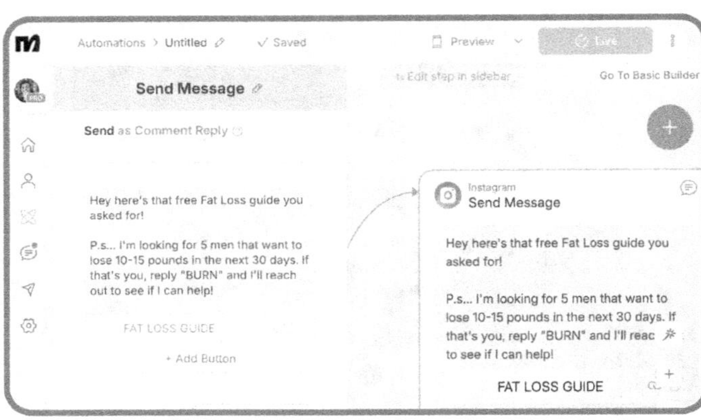

19. Go to the top of the page and select "Set live."

You just set up a Manychat automation for Instagram. You can do this for "Replies to Story" as well, and anyone who replies to your story with a specific keyword will receive the resource you tell Manychat to send them.

This is a great way to automate the first part of your lead generation process, and it's an absolute must for your coaching business because you never know which one of these posts is going to go viral. If you do have a post that goes viral and receives more than one thousand comments of people requesting your free resource and you *don't* have the auto-reply set up—that won't be fun for you.

I don't always attach a hard-sell CTA at the end of my Manychat messages; sometimes I just send the resource. But 50% of the time I will include that extra CTA.

Why?

Because I want to grow my coaching business. I know some people who reply for that free resource who are interested in working with me. So, I'd rather get those people to express interest and reply.

3. Instagram Livestreams to Podcasts

This is a cheat code that a lot of people don't do, and it blows my mind! It's low-hanging fruit. When I started my online coaching business, I listened to podcasts to identify competitors in the space and what they did. I found a guy named Sterling. He had a podcast with more than two hundred episodes that were specifically for online coaches.

During my research, I found that Sterling had a successful online business consulting the ideal client I wanted to speak to.

"Guess I got to start a podcast," I thought to myself.

Not only did I start a podcast, but I also decided to make it the No. 1 podcast for online fitness coaches—my ideal client demographic. Here's what I did to grow the podcast. I went live on Instagram five times a week and I recorded myself using Zoom and a professional podcast microphone. This allowed me to *record* the podcast at the same time. (You can add a second phone to your plan to get more leads. It costs you up to thirty dollars a month if you get the lowest possible plan, and then you can go live on two platforms at the same time.)

After I finished the podcast audio, I'd interact with my audience for a few minutes and ask them questions. Then I'd send traffic back to the podcast by saying, "By the way if you guys want more value make sure you check out the *Change Lives, Make Money* online trainer podcast."

My podcast started slow. I did it solo episodes got a few hundred downloads a month.

Since then, I've been podcasting for more than six years, and my podcast gets more than one hundred thousand downloads a month. It's become a primary vehicle for converting interested prospects into paying clients. It's also the place I send newer audience members to when they interact with my content but may not be fully ready to act on a coaching program.

I send them to the podcast because they can get so much value for free and they eventually warm up to the idea of becoming my client, so they can get results faster. Going live and recording podcast episodes was one of the single biggest things that took my business from zero to hero in one year.

If you don't have a podcast, start one. And if you *do* start a podcast, reach out to @travisbrown on Instagram.

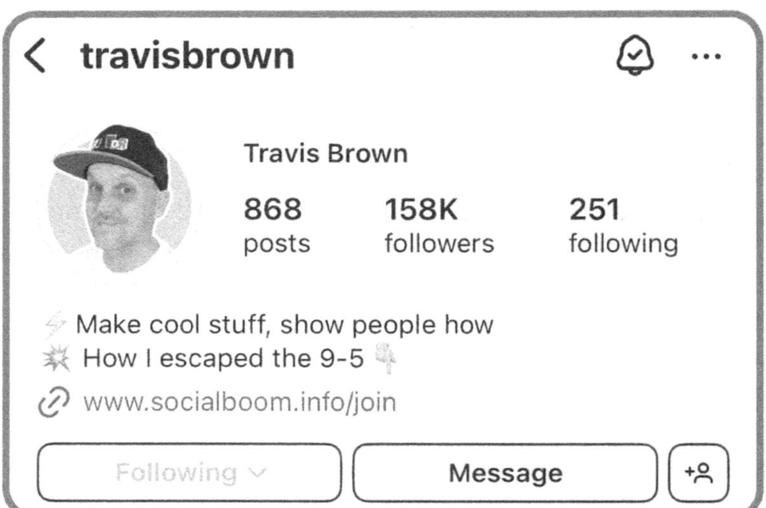

Tell him Brian Mark sent you. It's super affordable, he will get you on Apple, Spotify, and iTunes. He'll also help you design your cover art, your intro and outro music, tell you what podcasting gear you need to invest in, and brainstorm your first few episodes with you.

You're probably wondering, "What should I talk about on my livestreams or podcast?" Great question. Take what you're already talking about in your content and expand it for your livestreams. Here's how I like to structure my livestreams:

Livestream Structure

Intro: Welcome to [X] podcast (~ 30 seconds)

Set the Stage for [X] subject (~ 30–60 seconds)

Discuss three common mistakes made regarding [X] subject (~ 2–3 minutes)

Discuss three expected outcomes if they take [X] subject seriously: talk about benefits of listening to your advice and taking action (~ 2–3 minutes)

Tell a story of you or a client who successfully used [X] subject you're about to talk about (~ 2–3 minutes)

Give the actual value (anywhere from 5–15 minutes or longer)

End with a CTA to rate the podcast, leave a review, and share with their friends.

I recommend a schedule for your livestream that is based on the amount of time you can realistically commit to livestreams. So, go back to the Content Schedule chapter and make your plan using that information.

Even if you're not fully prepared to invest $1,500 to start your own podcast, you should still be regularly going live on Instagram. Livestreaming on Instagram and interacting with your audience is an easy way to take a lead from cold to hot because they'll see you're real person. Get out of your own way and hit that livestream button. Start talking to people. First, you'll have one person who tunes in. Then you'll get five people. That will grow to ten. And your live viewer numbers will continue to grow if you stay consistent.

3. Fourteen-Day Challenges

Fourteen-day challenges blew up both of businesses when they were first getting off the ground. The No. 1 determining factor in someone believing you know what you're talking about versus not, is social proof. When you're first getting started as an online fitness coach, you have zero social proof other than your own story of how you overcame your struggle. So, the best way to collect social proof when you're first getting started and you have a smaller business is to work for free to collect testimonials. I did this with my Aesthetic Nation fitness business. That was the primary conversion vehicle my new online coaches also did to grow their businesses. They did free, fourteen-day challenges every six weeks and they'd offer the challenge until their client roster was full.

They'd work with twenty people for free to help them lose weight, get results, and transform their life. In that short time period they'd help people see visible results and we were able to use their testimonials. Plus, they were also able to convert 10–20% of people from the free challenge to a high-ticket offer.

I did the same thing with PT Domination, my business consulting company for online personal trainers. I offered free, fourteen-day "get clients" challenges. In that short time period, I'd work with clients to help them set up their social media, create a few CTAs, help them with their DM scripts, and they'd see some results inside the container. Plus, I'd use that as social proof and be able to convert 10–20% of people from the challenge into my high-ticket offer.

So, it doesn't matter what industry you are in, running a free, fourteen-day challenge is an extremely effective way to generate leads and turn interested prospects into paying customers. We see this all the time. Most of your favorite apps offer a free, seven-day trial. Most gyms also include a week-long trial period.

Essentially, the trail gives you an opportunity to experience the app or experience the gym without paying for it, which makes you a lot more likely to justify the purchase of spending your hard-earned money. The same goes for your challenge. Give your prospects an opportunity to test out your service without paying for it.

Trust me, I've done every type of challenge, including six-week challenges, twenty-one-day challenges, seven-day challenges—you name it. The highest converting challenge for a smaller audience size is by far the free, fourteen-day challenge. This is especially true for coaches who are just getting started. It provides an opportunity to test your skills, practice for free, and collect social proof you can use in your marketing.

The fourteen-day challenge can be broken into four steps:

1. Marketing and Filling it
2. The Pre-Challenge Essentials
3. How to Run the Challenge
4. Converting from the Challenge

Let's dive into each of these steps, starting with the first one—marketing your challenge.

Step 1: Marketing the 14 Day Challenge

Great marketing is about joining the conversation happening in our prospects' brains. The best way to do that is to name your fourteen-day challenge something aspirational that they want, or something they want to get rid of. This would be a:

- Specific pain point
- Specific goal

Here are some examples:

Fitness: The 14-Day Visible Abs Challenge

Relationships: The 14-Day Better Husband Challenge

Sales: The 14-Day Elite Closer Challenge

Content Coaching: The 14-Day Go Viral Challenge

Mindset Coaching: The 14-Day Bulletproof Mentality Challenge

If the name of your challenge isn't attention-grabbing, no one will want to join the challenge. So, choose a name, then use ChatGPT to help you come up with ten to twenty other catchy names that are just like that using language your ideal client would use. Then, you can decide on the name that you're going to use for your challenge.

Marketing Materials

Once you decide on the name for your challenge, it's time to get to work on your marketing materials.

I'm going to assume that you're not a graphic designer reading this book, so I'm going to make this section simple.

Go to your Instagram Stories and choose a great photo of you. It needs to subconsciously communicate that you have the results people are looking to get from your challenge. Add that photo on your Instagram Stories then write: FREE 14-Day [Specific Niche] Challenge. That's the header information.

Beneath that text, you're going to add: I'm launching a FREE challenge for [specific niche] who want to [X specific result], [Y specific result] and [Z specific result].

Finally, you're going to add: Limited to 20 spots. First come, first serve. Starts on [date].

To design a carousel graphic for your fourteen-day challenge, you can use this format:

> **Slide 1:** FREE 14-Day [Challenge Name] Challenge Starts [Date] Limited to 20 people
>
> **Slide 2 text:** I'm looking for 20 committed [ideal clients] who want to get [X result] in the next 14 days.
>
> **Slide 3 text:** Who this is for (list three specific traits your avatar has in bullet points)
>
> **Slide 4 text:** What's included? (list the features and benefits of your program in bullet points)
>
> **Slide 5 text:** What are the expected outcomes? (Talk about client results that have happened in your program in bullet points)
>
> **Slide 6 text:** Give the program start date, number of open spots, and any other specific details needed
>
> **Slide 8 text:** Want to apply? Comment or DM me with the word CHALLENGE.

That's all you need in terms of front-end marketing material. For back-end material, you will need some a place to host the challenge. I recommend Facebook because that's what my clients have been building communities since 2014. A lot of coaches and trainers, however, have transitioned over to Skool as their primary community.

The platform you host your community on is irrelevant as long as you have a place to host live trainings and provide value to your group.

I prefer Facebook because most people are already using Facebook. If you decide to use Facebook, here's how you'll set up your group: Make a Facebook group for your free challenge. Add a cover photo that's a great photo of you, and add the name of your fourteen-day free challenge to the cover photo.

For your Facebook group description, ask ChatGPT to write a short description about your challenge.

All you need is a cover photo, group name, and description. Just like that you have your marketing materials set up for the back end.

For lead capture you're going to need to have a client application. To do this, create a free account on Typeform. Then create your own Typeform and design a welcome screen that has a photo of your challenge, the name of your challenge, and add the text "Limited to 20 people, first come first serve." Then add the following questions:

1. First and last name
2. Email address
3. Instagram username
4. What's your biggest struggle in [X] journey?
5. What's your No. 1 goal in [X] journey?
6. At the end of this 14-day challenge, I will present an opportunity to work with me for 90 days in my [name of program]. Would you be interested? (Yes/No answer)
7. Add your phone number if you'd like to schedule a free, 30-minute consult to create a gameplan for your specific goals. (Make this optional.)

The benefit of doing this is that anyone who leaves their phone number after answering "yes" to being pitched and leaving their phone number in the optional field just subconsciously agreed to the fact that you will pitch them. That tells you they're interested in coaching. Anyone who leaves their phone number at that point, you need to text them: "Hey [name], is this you?"

> *Prospect:* Yes, who's this.
>
> **You:** It's [name]. You just filled out the application for the 14-day challenge, and I saw you want to lose twenty pounds. That's awesome! Next step is to get you booked for your free, 30-minute consultation to create a gameplan for your goals.
>
> **You:** Send calendar link
>
> **You:** Book here. Spots are filling up quick! Once you're done, send me a screenshot so I know what time you pick, cool?

This allows you to book sales calls before your challenge even starts.

Promotion Schedule

Your promotion schedule for the fourteen-day challenge is simple. Begin marketing your challenge five to seven days before you launch your challenge. Post about it in your Instagram Stories and newsfeed like we previously discussed. You're also going to talk about it in your Instagram Stories in speaking videos.

Add a countdown timer to your Stories to show that the deadline is approaching. This creates urgency and scarcity. You'll also add a link to your Typeform application.

You want to post about your challenge every day until all twenty spots are filled.

Here's something to keep in mind. When you're just getting started, you may not be able to fill all your spots by posting on social media. You may have to send DMs to people who are following you, engaging with your content, on your friends list, and watching your stories. And ask them to join your challenge.

If you need to do this, here's the plan to send out one hundred DMs a day:

> **Message 1:** Hey [name], I'm launching a free fourteen-day [name] challenge on [date]. Interested?

About 20% of the people you message will reply. When they do, they'll either agree or they'll want more information. If they want more information you can reply:

> **You:** It's going to be fourteen days of live trainings, coaching, and support—all with the goal of getting you [X] result.
>
> **You:** Send them the Canva graphic or Instagram Story graphic you made
>
> **You:** The challenge starts [date]. Are you in?
>
> *Prospect:* They'll likely agree to join
>
> **You:** Awesome
>
> **You:** Now you'll send the Typeform application link
>
> **You:** Go ahead and fill out this form to save your spot. It'll only take you two minutes. The challenge is filling up quick. When you're done with the form, come back here and say "DONE." Then, I can confirm you on my end. Cool?

Continue doing this until you get twenty people registered for your challenge.

Once people are registered, send them the Facebook group link and make sure they request to join the group. Don't add anyone to the group until the first day of the challenge. Let the requests build up and approve everyone at once.

2. Pre-Challenge Essentials

High-Converting Challenge Psychology

To run a successful fourteen-day, free challenge you need to understand challenge psychology. People follow other people's social behaviors, which is why when a riot breaks out in a city, people go insane. We're herd creatures. It's also why stock markets are predictable. People make trades in the stock market, and people are predictable. Understanding this psychology will allow us to use it to our advantage.

In order to illustrate this next point, I want you to imagine that you get invited to a party. You walk through the front doors of the house where the party is. You see one person, the host's mom, sitting on the couch eating chips.

You were told the party was going to be a slamming, but the only slamming happening is the host's mom slamming chips back on the couch. How likely are you to stay at the party and dance?

Very unlikely!

Let's say, however, you walk through the front doors of the house and you see thirty people. Everyone's dancing, singing, and having a good time. What's the likelihood you'll stick around?

Very likely!

People follow other people's social behavior, which is why you need to set up your Facebook group in a way that gets the party going and keeps it alive throughout the challenge.

With challenges, they're always going to lose engagement as the challenge goes on. Why? Because it's free, and some people value what they didn't pay for. They say they want it, but they don't hold any value to it, because it's free.

If you understand this, then you understand your job as the group leader is to get the engagement as high as possible to start. If it starts super high to start, then it'll finish high. But if the group engagement starts average, it's going to finish off low. If your group engagement starts off low, it's going to end quiet as a ghost town.

So, here's how to set up your challenge to make sure people stay engaged and participate, so they get results and you get social proof and sign clients.

Create a Welcome Post for Your Challenge

The welcome post for your challenge should be a short two- to three-minute video. You'll explain the rules of the challenge, welcome your challengers and tell them they just made the best decision of their lives by choosing to sign up for the challenge. Inform them about the structure of the challenge, which includes two live trainings a week and pre-recorded trainings to be completed as homework during the challenge. Inform new challengers that clients who achieve the best results are those who engage, ask questions, and post in the group. Encourage them to utilize the group to its full potential to obtain the best outcomes. Finally, instruct new group members to comment on the welcome post with an introduction, their No. 1 goal for the challenge, and why they're excited for the challenge.

Pin the welcome post to the top of the group so it's the first thing people see when they join.

Approve Everyone In the Group at One Time

You're going to let the requests for your group build up until you hit all twenty spots requested, then you'll let everyone in at once. This way, the party starts for everyone at the same time. It'll allow your challenge to start with extremely high engagement.

Message Everyone a Quick Voice Note 30 Minutes Ahead of Request Approvals

Here's what you can say, "Hey, what's going on [name]! Hope you're having the best day of your entire life. Just wanted to let you know that I'm accepting you into the group in 30 minutes. Once I do, make sure you watch the introduction video and introduce yourself in the comments! Excited to have you on board."

By doing these three things, you'll ensure your group starts off with fire engagement, which will lead to a higher converting challenge.

Setting Up a High-Converting Challenge

Before you start your challenge, you need to make sure you have your schedule dialed in. In order to make your schedule, you need to identify four or five steps you can give your ideal client that will help them see visible results in a fourteen-day period.

As a fitness coach, you could give provide a workout program for two weeks that helps challengers lose two to ten pounds. As a sales coach you could teach how to pre-frame a call, how to do discovery on a call, how to price present, and how to overcome objections. As a content coach, you could teach how to create strong hooks, how to perform content research, how to write scripts, and how to audit content.

No matter your niche, create tangible trainings you can give to your challengers that will help them get results. That's how you're going design the trainings that go into your challenge.

I recommend doing two or three livestreams or coaching calls a week for the duration of the challenge. In one you'll teach and give homework. In the other, you'll do a Q&A on a zoom call.

Another successful way to run a challenge is to do two trainings a week: one on Monday and one on Thursday. In both, you give value-based information on your specific subject along with actionable homework for them to do to see results.

When it comes to fourteen-day challenges, keep the value simple. One time, I ran a twenty-one-day challenge and I had 650 people in the challenge. I wrote a thirty-page eBook ahead of time and thought I'd give the group the entire blueprint to get incredible results. I converted one person from the challenge.

I learned that overwhelmed prospects don't make purchases.

When I do a challenge now, I focus on fifteen- to twenty-minute trainings and how I can give a ton of value on a very specific issue. Then, within that very specific issue, I give actionable homework challengers must post in the group once they complete it.

Livestream Structure

I use the same structure for challenge livestreams as I do for my podcasts; the only difference is I offer a one-hundred-dollar Amazon gift card away during my fourteen-day challenges.

The way I have people enter to win the gift card is tell them to screenshot the training, post it to their Instagram Stories, and tag my Instagram account with the phrase, "Learning from BMark."

That gets ten to twenty people sharing about me on their Instagram Stories every day for fourteen days. I can re-use those posts as social proof, and I can share their stories and gain exposure from their audience. From that giveaway, I choose one person who shares a screenshot every day, and that person gets the one-hundred-dollar gift card.

Livestream Script

Intro, welcome to the training (~ 30 seconds)

Set the Stage for the Subject (~ 30–60 seconds)

Explain how to win a $100 Amazon gift card

Talk about the three common mistakes people make and the negative consequences of those mistakes regarding [specific subject] (2–3 minutes)

Talk about the benefits of listening to your advice and three expected outcomes in they take [specific subject] seriously and take action (2–3 minutes)

Tell a story of you or a client who successfully used [specific subject] you're about to talk about (2–3 minutes)

Give the value (5–15 minutes or longer)

End with a CTA and give specific homework they can do.

I recommend pre-scheduling all your Facebook posts for the week. You want to keep the group engaged, and you can do a lot of the work ahead of time and set up your challenge for success.

Recommended Posting Schedule

Week 1

- Monday: Livestream or Zoom
- Tuesday: Homework check-in
    - Your homework from yesterday's call was to complete [X]. How's it going? Comment and let me know
- Wednesday: Winning Wednesday
    - Tell me a win you've experienced this week because of what you've learned!
- Thursday: Livestream or Zoom
- Friday: Post a Social Proof Post of one of your clients

Week 2

- Monday: Livestream or Zoom
- Tuesday
    - I'm looking for five [avatar] that want to get [specific result] in [specific time frame]. If that's you, comment [keyword] below
- Wednesday: Winning Wednesday
    - Tell me a win you've experienced this week because of what you've learned!
- Thursday: Livestream or Zoom

- Friday
    - Social Proof Post Template (see Chapter 4) with CTA
    - You have a successful fourteen-day challenge.

3. How to Run Your Fourteen-Day Challenge

We already discussed the importance of getting everyone to introduce themselves right away in the comments of the Facebook group. If anyone doesn't introduce themselves, make sure to message them and get them to engage. Remember, your goal is to get the party bumping right away.

Beyond that, here's how to successfully run your fourteen-day challenge. First, set a pre-defined time to go live every day. This will help your challengers build that time into their schedules, so they don't miss a call. Second, make sure as many people as possible show up to your live trainings. The more people who show up, the more money you'll make. Third, if you give access to a portal of any type (sales training, content coaching, or fitness app) then you need to make sure are many people log into the app as possible.

It's not going to be perfect, but go above and beyond to get as many people access as possible because the more people who use the information you give them, the more social proof you'll generate and the more money that you'll make.

Regarding your Facebook group, make sure you reply to every comment and every post in your group. I recommend spending twenty minutes each morning, afternoon, and evening responding to comments and posts. Your next $3,000 to $10,000 is in that Facebook group—treat it like so.

One hour before every coaching call, send a personal message to every person in your challenge reminding them about your upcoming coaching call. Doing so ensures that you have the most amount of people show up to the coaching call, which means you'll get more social proof, more transformations, and close more challengers.

Your goal running your challenge is to give as much value as possible, in the simplest and most digestible format as possible. That way people can take your information and see results in fourteen days.

4. Converting from the Fourteen-Day Challenge

This part's fun and it's easy, too. The first opportunity you have to convert challengers is before your challenge even starts. We talked about how to reach out via text before your challenge starts. In addition to that, have a list of every challenger who is in your fourteen-day challenge and aim to have one daily interaction with them.

I keep a list of all my challengers, I try to do one touch point every day. I spend 20 minutes going through the list. I might open Facebook Messenger on the first day of the challenge and send everyone a message to encourage them to engage.

On the second day, I may ask some participants if they caught the coaching call. If they did, I'll ask what they learned. For day three, I may comment on a few people's social media posts. You get the idea. Maintain relationships with your participants throughout the challenge.

Doing so organically will lead some of them to book a call with you. When that happens, book the damn call. You do not need to wait until the end the challenge to sell. The challenge is a lead magnet to attract people who need your help. Some people in your challenge are going to be hot leads and ready to go from the first day. They reached out because they want to get the result you advertised. Book the call.

Other opportunities to convert will come when you post your "five guys" post during the challenge.

At the end of your final livestream, you'll also say, "That brings us to the end of this challenge. Some of you may be interested in one-on-one coaching and continuing to learn. If that's you, drop a 'Hell yes' in the comments! After this livestream, I'll reach out to each of you individually to set a free, thirty-minute consult to talk about your goals."

You'll get the most traffic for bookings at the end of the challenge. You're going to send a direct message to every person who participated in the challenge, and say,

> **You:** Hey [name]! I'm reaching out because the challenge is over and to celebrate the end, I'm offering a 30-minute, free strategy session to come up with a gameplan that'll move you toward your [X] goal. You in?
>
> *Participant:* They'll say sure
>
> **You:** Perfect, let me grab my calendar link
>
> **You:** Share calendar link
>
> **You:** Go ahead and book through my calendar link. Spots fill up quick. Send me a screenshot when you book. Cool?

Following that script, you'll take people from a complete stranger on social media, warm them up to the point where they get value from you and they're interested in purchasing, and then you'll convert them into a phone call where you'll be able to pitch and sell your program.

5. Flash Sales

This strategy should be used sparingly—I'd say maximum once a month. You can make this one of your hard-sell CTAS that you post on Monday.

Everyone loves a good deal and you can use that to your advantage by doing flash sales for your coaching program. Here's the rule with flash sales though. Twenty-five percent off is the max you should go, unless you're doing very high volume—aka thousands of leads a month. The flash sale price only applies to people who pay in full. To run a successful flash sale, you must understand the Because Effect.

This effect is based on research by a social psychologist named Ellen Langer. She found that people are more likely to comply with a request when a reason is given—even if it's not a strong reason.

Why?

People are wired to accept reasons without overanalyzing them. When people hear the word "Because" or they read a sentence that justifies a flash sale, they are more likely to act.

You don't have to use the word "because." You can imply it with reason.

Here's an example: When I reached 250,000 Instagram followers, I held a 25% off flash sale.

So, I shared a post that said, "I just hit 250,000 Instagram followers and to celebrate, I am offering 25% off all business coaching programs for online fitness coaches. I will help you go viral, sign clients and make an extra $10,000 online. DM me 25 OFF for more information."

You'll see that I gave a specific reason why I launched the flash sale. Since I gave a logical reasoning behind the sale, my audience was significantly more likely to take action on the sale.

To add the elements of urgency and scarcity to your flash sale, you need to add some elements to your Instagram Story that make it more valuable. For instance, you can add a countdown timer to the flash sale post to signal when the offer expires. That will encourage people to take action.

Regarding your CTAs, you need to have the CTA geared toward your audience size.

If you're under 10,000 followers, then you should have people vote on a poll if they are interested in your flash sale. This way, you collect as many leads as possible if you're under 10,000 followers, which is why you get people to vote. It's easy to vote.

If you're over 10,000 followers, then you want to use the direct message a keyword CTA. Between the 10,000 and 100,000 follower mark, you should have people DM you because you'll typically get more serious people DM you. This is because there's more resistance to DM rather than tap a voting poll on a Story. Not to mention, when you have 10,000 or more followers, you may have one thousand people vote on your poll.

If you're over 100,000 followers, and you don't have a virtual assistant (VA), you should have people apply for your coaching offer right away through a Typeform. On your Instagram Story, include a link to your Typeform application. Then add this text: "Hey, I'm getting hundreds of DMs about the flash sale and I don't know who's serious and who's not. So, if you're serious, take two minutes and fill out a client application if you want to get [X] result. Then DM me DONE so I know you've completed it."

Your Instagram account is a marketing funnel, so when you increase the volume on the funnel you need to optimize the way you capture your hottest leads. If you're over 100,000 followers, getting your leads to fill out a Typeform right away from a DM CTA will allow you to look through the Typeforms to find your hot leads instead of having to scroll through thousands of messages to see who's serious.

6. The Magnetic Giveaway

This is probably one of my favorite ways to generate leads, and once you learn this strategy you can't forget it. This strategy is best done once every three months because it's extremely effective. If you do it too much, your audience will get wise and won't reply or enter. The strategy is simple. You're going to give away a $1,500 program (or the value of your service) in return for entering a giveaway. Anyone who enters your giveaway will be a potential lead you can message afterward and offer incentives to join your coaching program if they *don't* win your giveaway.

You're going to use the same "Because" philosophy we spoke about in the last section, and you need to have a specific reason to do the giveaway.

Is it because it's the first day of summer? Because you hit 10k followers? Because you've been in business for one year? Because it's Christmas? Because it's your birthday?

Find a reason to do your giveaway.

For the last magnetic giveaway I did, I had 350 entries and I booked seventy calls after the giveaway ended. I generated more than $100,000 in revenue from this one strategy and one Instagram post.

> Advertise on the front end that you're giving away a [$X] program because [X].
>
> Give the rules to enter the giveaway.
>
> Collect all the data from the entrants for the giveaway.
>
> Promote the giveaway for 48 hours.
>
> Announce the winner publicly.
>
> Then, immediately convert the people who didn't win the giveaway into leads.

Here's an example of the slides of one of my most recent giveaways.

Here's the exact script I used, but you can modify it for your own offer:

> $6,000 Business Coaching Program Giveaway
>
> We just celebrated six years in business! And to celebrate, I am giving away the opportunity for one lucky online coach or aspiring online coach to

go through a 12-month mentorship program with us designed to make you at least $5,000–$10,000 per month for the low cost of completely free.

Complete these steps:

1. Comment WINNER on this post
2. Tag 3 personal trainer friends in the comments
3. Fill out the form that I send you over DMs

I will choose one person who completes all three steps!

Bonus entry for $500 cash for one person who shares this post to their Instagram Stories!

Entries will close on Monday @ 8:30 a.m. PST.

I'll announce the winner Monday @ 9 PST on Instagram Stories!

And... GO!

therealbrianmark 2w
1/5
350k Follower
15,000
GIVEAWAY
YEP, YOU READ THAT RIGHT.
$18K GIVEAWAY. SWIPE FOR DETAILS
>>>>>

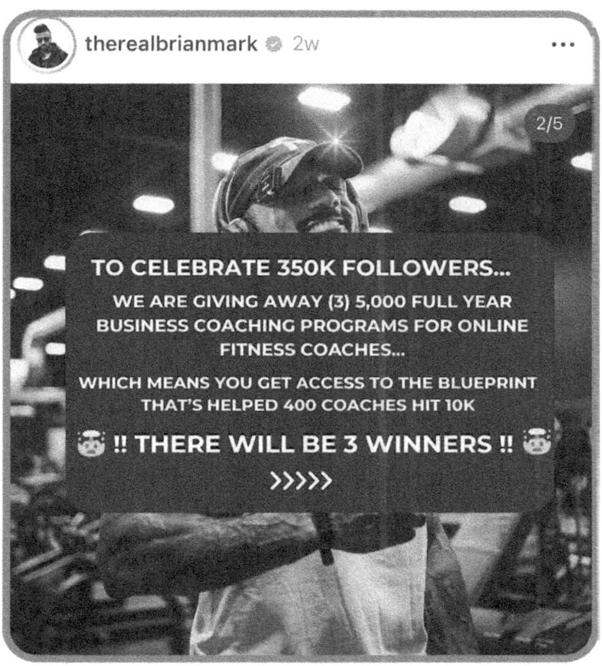
therealbrianmark 2w
2/5
TO CELEBRATE 350K FOLLOWERS...
WE ARE GIVING AWAY (3) 5,000 FULL YEAR BUSINESS COACHING PROGRAMS FOR ONLINE FITNESS COACHES...
WHICH MEANS YOU GET ACCESS TO THE BLUEPRINT THAT'S HELPED 400 COACHES HIT 10K
!! THERE WILL BE 3 WINNERS !!
>>>>>

therealbrianmark 2w
COMPLETE THESE 3 STEPS...
1) COMMENT "350K"
2) FILL OUT THE ENTRY FORM THAT GETS SENT TO YOUR DMS
3) TAG 3 FRIENDS IN THE COMMENTS (UNLIMITED TAGS, UNLIMITED ENTRIES)
BONUS: SHARE THE FIRST SLIDE TO YOUR INSTAGRAM STORIES FOR AN ADDITIONAL CHANCE TO WIN !!

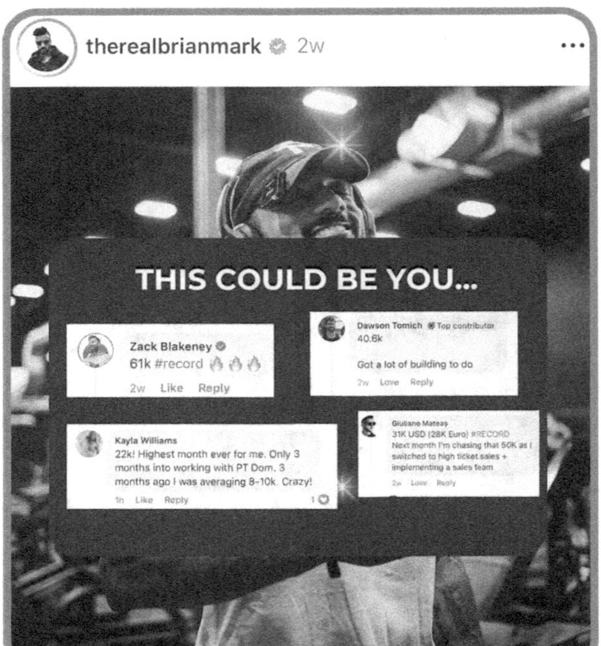
therealbrianmark 2w
THIS COULD BE YOU...
Zack Blakeney
61k #record
2w Like Reply
Dawson Tomich Top contributor
40.6k
Got a lot of building to do
2w Love Reply
Kayla Williams
22k! Highest month ever for me. Only 3 months into working with PT Dom. 3 months ago I was averaging 8-10k. Crazy!
1h Like Reply 1
Giuliano Mateaş
31K USD (28K Euro) #RECORD
Next month I'm chasing that 50K as I switched to high ticket sales + implementing a sales team
2w Love Reply

♡ 336 💬 514

Liked by **coachleticialockhart** and **others**

therealbrianmark 15,000 350K BIZ COACHING PROGRAM GIVEAWAY 🔥🔥

We just hit 350k Followers and to CELEBRATE... 🎉

We are giving away (3) FULL 5,000 Year Long Mentorship Programs to (3) lucky Online Coaches / Aspiring online coaches who want to scale their business

All for the low cost of COMPLETELY... FREE 🤯🤯

You'l get:

✅ Access to the blueprint that's helped over 10,000 coaches in the last 6 years quit their jobs and go full time online

✅ 3 Live Coaching calls per week designed to help you go viral, attract more clients, book more sales calls and earn 5-10k / mo

✅ Access to the PT Dom Community where we have over 1,500 active students sharing wins, secrets, insights to help you grow faster

HOW TO ENTER: Complete these steps... 👇

1️⃣ Comment "350K" on this post 👇
2️⃣ Tag at least 3 Personal Trainer friends in the comments
3️⃣ Fill out the form that I DM you to complete your entry.

🎉 BONUS ENTRY: Share the first slide to your Instagram Stories for an additional chance to win!

We will choose THREE people who complete all 3 of these steps! And we will help you make 50-150k this year with your online fitness business. 🐺🐺

Entries will CLOSE at Sunday, March 23 @ 11:00am PST ‼️

I'll announce the winner Sunday March 23 @ 12:00pm PST on Instagram Stories.

And... GO!! 👇 #DOMINATE

When someone comments the word "WINNER" on your post, I want you to send them a Typeform application to officially cement their entry into the giveaway.

You're going to use the Typeform to collect their information to ensure you can contact the prospects who don't win the giveaway.

https://brianmark.typeform.com/dec24giveaway

Follow the exact questions and use this Canva graphic on your giveaway and you're good to go.

When done correctly, this giveaway will get you dozens of leads through your giveaway. Your goal is to promote the giveaway for 48 hours and collect as many entries as you can. You can even message leads and prospects and make them aware that you are doing a giveaway. Use a script like this, "Hey [name], hope you're doing well! Just wanted you to know that

I'm doing a massive giveaway on my page, thought you might be interested!"

All the magic will happen on the day of your giveaway, so make sure you're ready to rock and roll.

You'll want to announce your giveaway winner during the morning; I recommend between 8 and 9 a.m. As soon as you announce your giveaway winner, I want you to message every person who entered your giveaway with a personal voice or video recording. Here's what you can say:

> Hey! What's up [name]! Hope you're having a great day. I'm sending you a personal note to let you know you didn't win the official giveaway. However, I loved your entry because of [X specific thing from their entry], so I'm giving you a $500 credit toward my coaching program. All you have to do to claim the credit is reply "hell yes," and I'll get you set up!

If you have fifty entries, you're going to send fifty personal messages. And you're going to send them all as soon as you announce your giveaway winner.

Psychologically, you don't want the people who didn't win your giveaway to find out from your post because then they'll be disappointed. You want them to find out from a personal message you send them. That way, even though they're disappointed they didn't win, they're still going to be excited they won a credit to your program. You'll get a bunch of people who reply back with "hell yes!"

From that point, you're going to follow this script:

> **You:** I love it! Next step is to get you set up on a quick 15–30-minute call. We'll talk about your No. 1 goal in your [niche] right now, your main struggle, and set up with the credit.
>
> **You:** Send calendar link

> **You:** Go ahead and select a time from my calendar that works for you. Spots fill up quick. Once you've booked, send me a screenshot so I can confirm on my end. Cool?

This is the *exact* strategy that's generated more than seventy sales calls for me and $100,000 in revenue.

7. Other Ways to Get Clients

The best way to generate leads for your online business is through Instagram Stories. You need to consistently be documenting your life and walking the walk on your Instagram Stories so your audience has something to aspire to, someone to look up to, and someone to be more like.

That being said, when referring to client acquisition strategies, you need to document all of the successful client testimonials in your coaching program over and over again. Your audience needs to see what happens when they listen to your advice.

Show clients who started out with you with [X] problem and now have [X] result. You can share before and after photos. You can share screenshots of client wins in series.

Here are a few more examples:

- Show screenshots of wins
- Show screenshots of graphs.
- Show screenshots of stripe accounts.
- Show screenshots of before and after.
- Share testimonial videos from clients.

Whatever you choose, do it over and over again.

Here's why it's important to do fourteen-day challenges to collect testimonials: You don't have testimonials when you first start, so the best way to get them is to work for free to collect them.

As a part of your ongoing marketing strategy, you need to document social proof on your Instagram Stories every day. Not a day goes by that I don't post client results on my story. It's why I generate more than three hundred sales calls a month from my Instagram. My audience *knows* what happens when they follow my advice. They get the results that my clients get.

When you share your client stories, say, "My clients win," and show a bunch of screenshots stacked on top of one another showing client wins.

Million Dollar Mastermind in Feb..
Kenny Dussault
49.1k MASSIVE record.
Spent the month focused on delegating and creating clarity in my team.
Biggest lesson? Everyone needs to be crystal clear on their roles and responsibilities.

Million Dollar Mastermind in Feb..
Erin Avery
$47.4k not a record but consistently near that mark which feels good. Making some big changes to my systems this month and adding to my team again

Million Dollar Mastermind in Feb..
Jonathan Ramirez
31k #Record
2nd month back to back at 30k for the first time ever.

Million Dollar Mastermind in Feb..
Brandon Johnson
32,000. #Record

Million Dollar Mastermind in Feb..
Kevin Wu
39.5k
had a dry period from Feb 6-20 with only 1 mid ticket sale. Feeling it for March though

Million Dollar Mastermind in Feb..
Steven Y Migridichian
43k...no record month first time in 7 months. Time to GO HARD. We're scaling the ads up.

Million Dollar Mastermind in Feb..
Trent Harrison All-star contributor
$174k in February

Million Dollar Mastermind in Feb..
Hallie Hobday
Flying first class on emirates to Milan
Flying on this exact plane in first class has been a DREAM of mine since I was a little girl and I had no idea I would be able to do it this early
This lifestyle would not be possible without this group! Our life has changed forever and I am so grateful
Also if you aren't putting all of your business expenses on the Amex platinum card and earning points for free travel then what r u doing - I paid $210 total for Hector and I for these seats

Million Dollar Mastermind in Feb..
Erin Avery
I've been waiting to make this post. Bought my first home. I still can't freaking believe it. This goal felt sooo out of reach for so long (especially living in Orange County). When I started with the CLA I was barely making 2k a month and living paycheck to paycheck. Now my team is about to cross 50k. This community is seriously so crazy and I'm insanely grateful to be a part of it. Huge thank you to everyone in here
See the trend?
Dm me "10k" if you want results like this

You can also add CTAs to these social proof stories. Add something like, "If you want results like this, DM me [KEYWORD] for more information."

If you want to sign clients from Instagram, then you have to document successful client transformations on your Instagram Stories every day.

SUMMARY

Wow, we packed a *ton* in this chapter! I hope you have enough ammunition to take immediate action, start signing clients, and make money right away. If your business is ever not generating enough revenue, re-read this chapter and choose one of the seven client acquisition strategies and apply it to your business.

In the next chapter, I'm how to book sales calls from your direct messages.

CHAPTER 9

USING DIRECT MESSAGES TO BOOK FIVE TO TEN SALES CALLS A WEEK

Oh boy, buckle up, this is going to be fun! By the end of this chapter, you're going to have a thorough understanding of how to properly use Instagram direct messages (DMs) to book calls, make sales, and grow your business to levels you have a hard time imagining right now. Before I get into the DM theory I want to give credit to Taki Moore, who I learned this tactic from. I compiled expert advice I've received during the last seven years of being in business, and built my expertise based off the foundations Taki gave me.

UNDERSTANDING DMS

First things first, you must understand the nature of the platforms you are on and why Instagram is by far the king when it comes to converting interested prospects into paying clients.

TikTok is great for getting more exposure, but the messaging feature sucks. No one uses it. A podcast is great for nurturing leads, however, people can't message you from the podcast platform. YouTube is good for sharing long-form content and nurturing prospects, but again, in terms of a lead generation platform—no bueno. Listen, Facebook is great and a lot of my business comes from Facebook. The problem with Facebook, however, is that they have message restrictions on personal accounts, and they are way more intense about those restrictions than Instagram. That creates a bottleneck in scaling your business.

Now, LinkedIn, I personally used the platform for more than two years to grow my business and I never saw as much return on investment (ROI) from it as I did from Instagram. The messaging platform is useful, and you can grow your business on LinkedIn using the same DM theory and framework I'm about to give you, but Instagram remains "King of the DMs." People are on Instagram to scroll through social media, but people are also on Instagram to interact with other humans. That's why the platform offers people tags, where you can tag a friend in your Stories and they see it in the app's message inbox. It's also why we have the messaging feature; it provides us all with instant access to brands and personalities we may have never had access to before. Take my wifey, Kirsten Mark, for example. She had access to Justin Bieber's DM's and sent him one hundred messages over the course of two years—just hoping he'd reply. He never did (lucky me), but direct messaging gave her the ability to send message to the Biebs. All jokes aside, Instagram DMs are the absolute GOAT when it comes to generating sales online.

And here's the thing, marketing continues to evolve. People are sick of the whole song and dance of being sent to a landing page to be sold something. They want to talk to humans.

I don't know about you, but when I call my bank and I help with something, I repeat "Talk to human" until I'm able to communicate with a real person instead of an automated teller. We all want to talk to other people, and DMs give us the ability to connect with our audience.

But how do you use Instagram DMs to make money? First, you need to change how you view direct messages. Do you see direct messages as a way to generate new business? Until you view Instagram DMs through that lens, you're going to avoid sending DMs. "I don't want to be salesy," is the excuse I get all the time from people who also want to grow and scale their businesses on social media.

You're viewing every single person on your social media as a potential transaction. Instead, you should simply see every person on social media as a human you should build a relationship with. This change in belief will serve you one hundred times better than viewing people as dollar signs, and it's going to make it significantly easier for you to generate authentic conversations that build relationships.

UNDERSTANDING THE PURPOSE OF THE DM'S

The purpose of direct messages is simple—to build relationships. You want to establish relationships with people who are in your audience and interact with your content. You want to establish relationships with people who are on your follower list because they made the decision to follow you on social media. Build relationships.

I have one simple belief when it comes to direct messaging: I *never* send cold DMs. A cold DM is a direct message to someone who has never seen me on social media, has never interacted with my content in any way, isn't following me online, and has no idea who I am.

It's rude, so I don't do it. Imagine walking up to a stranger and saying, "Hey Bob, want to buy from me?"

That's why 99% of online coaches fail. They take a transactional approach to social media and they send DMs to people they've never provided any value to and they wonder why they don't get responses.

Your goal is to give *so much* value to people for free that they could get results without ever hiring you. Build your brand presence, your authority, and your credibility through free content. Then, because you built credibility through your free content, when you send messages people are more likely to be receptive to you and what you have to say.

That's the game I like to play. Be the honey, not the bee.

HOW DO YOU APPROACH DMS?

Start the conversation. I'm going to give you a few different conversation openers you can use.

- Hey [name], just want to say thanks for the follow. Are you on a fitness journey or just enjoying the content?
- Hey [name], just wanted to say thanks for engaging with the content. I appreciate you.
- Hey [name], thanks for all the love on my content. How long have you been following me for?

JUST SAY HI

Your goal is to say "hi" to a minimum of twenty people every day. As your audience size increases, the number of people you send messages to every day should also increase. I start three to four hundred new conversations every day with people who interact with my content, follow me, watch my Stories, etc.

THEN WHAT?

Gauge the temperature of your prospects. You're going to do this for every lead based on two criteria.

Time of Response + Length of Response = Temperature of Lead

These criteria will show you if you have a cold, warm, or hot lead. Take a look:

- No Response + No Response = Cold lead; leave them alone.
- Takes a long time to respond + Short Response = Cold lead.
- Responds quickly)+ Short Response = Warm lead
- Takes a long time to respond + Long response = Warm lead
- Responds Quickly + Long Response = Hot lead

What you do with each of your leads should be 100% predicated on the temperature of the lead. If someone is a cold lead, they are going to require more conversation and relationship building. Asking where they're from, how long they've been following you, and their backstory are all valid questions to get them to open up and be receptive to the conversation with you.

If someone is a warm lead, this means that they either respond quickly but their responses are short or they take a long time to respond but their answers are longer. With a warm lead, you'll be able to move the conversation along quicker to get to the DM script below.

Finally, if someone is a hot lead, that essentially means they are sending you love letters or expressing a ton of interest. With hot leads, you can cut straight to the point and move through the DM script quickly to book a call.

When it comes to the DMs, you also must have the understanding of where people are in their customer journey. If you send a DM to someone who watches your Instagram Stories, sure they're consuming your content and part of your audience, but on a scale of one to ten do you know how ready they are to buy? It's probably a lot less likely than someone who votes on your Story Poll for a Five Guys post.

Have the self-awareness to know where your prospects are in their buying journey. If the lead came from a "Like" on your Instagram post or they're a new follower, assume that they're likely a colder lead. If the lead comes from a Story poll response, an incoming DM, or an application for your coaching program, then you can assume that lead is going to be a warm or hot lead. I'm not going to tell you not to sell to cold leads or that warm leads don't still need to be nurtured, but I want you to have the awareness to know how to handle each conversation.

WHAT TO DO BASED ON LEAD TEMPERATURES

If a lead is cold, there's a small likelihood that they will book a call or buy anything from you. So, continue to nurture the relationship and show them that you care about them, but remain focused on building the relationship.

Here are a few ways to nurture a cold lead with questions:

1) What's your story? What got you into [your journey]?
2) What's your main goal for 2025? Mine is ...
3) How long have you been following me?
4) I wrote a free eBook about fat loss that I wrote for my clients. It's helped a ton of people [Get specific result]. Mind if I send it over? ☺
5) Which of my content do you resonate with the most?

BUILD RELATIONSHIPS WITH WARM LEADS

If you have a warm lead, the likelihood that they will book a call or buy anything from you is much higher. So, you need to get enough data from the conversation to offer some help and guidance. This DM script is perfect for this:

You: What's your number one struggle in [specific journey]?

Prospect: Gives a one-word reply.

You: Tell me a little bit more about that, what do you mean by [this] specifically? Can you expand on that?

BOOK HOT LEADS

If your lead is hot, there's a very high likelihood that they will book a call or buy from you. You don't want to waste time with these prospects; they are already sending long messages and replying fast. Your goal is to book a call with these people as soon as possible because hot leads feel the *emotions* of buying. If you take too long to book the call, your lead can cool off. Use my DM script and get through it as soon as possible. If your lead is begging for help, skip parts of the DM script and jump to offering a free call. "Tell you what, why don't we set up a quick 15-minute call? We can talk about your No. 1 struggle in your [X journey], your biggest goal, and I'll give you a gameplan to help you get there. Are you up for that?"

STEP BY STEP LEAD GENERATION

Don't waste your time on bad leads. Your goal is to find Five-Star Prospects, which are leads that are friendly and cooperative, willing to engage in dialogue, know what they want, know when they want it, and want some help.

A Five-Star Prospect is:

1) **Friendly and co-operative:** If you send a message to someone and they send a rude message back, they're out. If they get sassy and rude, they're gone. Only engage with people who are friendly and co-operative.

2) **Willing to engage in dialogue**: If you send a message to someone and they do not reply, don't spend time following up and trying to engage. They don't want to engage in dialogue, so don't waste time trying to convince someone to engage with you.

3) **Decisive**: If a prospect is unsure of what they want when you message with them, and they are unsure of their goals and are wishy-washy about their aspirations—they will

also be a wishy-washy client. Save yourself time and energy and don't engage with people who aren't decisive.

4) **Ready to go:** Someone who knows what they want and *when* they want—that's a great client in the making. The more specific the better! When someone knows what they want, it gives them a burning desire to reach their goals as soon as possible.

5) **Willing to accept help:** The only way to figure out if someone wants help solving their problem is to ask. So, ask them if they want help. If they do, book the call.

Lead Generation to Book Sales Calls with Prospective Clients

Your goal is to find people who are Five-Star Prospects and book them for a fifteen- to thirty-minute phone call. During the call, you'll figure out if they're a good fit for your program. Your goal is to book one call every day from your lead generation efforts.

DM SCRIPT FOR FIVE-STAR PROSPECTS

In order to identify whether or not someone is a Five-Star Prospect, I want you to use my DM script to book qualified sales calls in your calendar. A word of caution, don't sound like a robot when you follow this script. Your prospect will sense that you're reading from a script, and they'll stop responding. To avoid sounding like a robot, here's a chat flow to follow and embody:

Three-Step Framework

1) **Validate** their response: Use words like

    a. Perfect
    b. Makes sense
    c. I get it
    d. Agreed

e. Cool
f. Okay
g. Awesome
h. I love it

2) **Relate** to them as an authority: Say things like:

a. Many of my clients felt the same way
b. My previous clients struggled with that as well
c. That used to be a problem from my clients
d. That would be frustrating
e. That's a pretty common problem

3) **Lean** in to uncover more: Ask questions like:

a. What have you tried so far?
b. What's the biggest thing you struggle with regarding your goal?
c. What's your main goal for your [X journey]?
d. What's your No. 1 goal for [X journey]?
e. What are three things you need to do in the next 90 days to reach your goal?

This is great, right? But you're probably wondering "Where are we finding these leads to start conversations with?" Here are seven places on Instagram to generate leads from:

1. **Instagram DMs** (very hot): This is the No. 1 place where your leads are the hottest. We want to get people into your DMs. Anyone who takes time to send you a direct message is extremely interested in communicating with you. The goal is to take that communication and turn it into a phone call.

2. **Instagram Stories poll responders** (hot): These people may not have it in them to message you, but they're interested enough to vote in your polls. As a content creator, you have to speak to your audience and give them what they want. The more you do that, the more positive

responses you'll get on your polls when you share them. Your goal is to start a conversation with people in your Stories and move them toward the chat flow.

3. **Instagram post commenters** (warm): These people are warm leads who need a bit of nurturing. I don't recommend opening with a lead-gen-type message right away. Long-term, that's a less effective strategy. Instead, message them about something they saw on your profile to start a conversation. Here's one of my favorites that's worked well: Hey [name]! I really appreciate you commenting on my last post. What's something that stood out the most?

4. **Instagram post likes** (lukewarm): These prospects will also need a bit of nurturing. I recommend visiting their profile and engaging on a few of their photos—leave a few comments and like some posts. you're playing the long game, and the more you like and engage with people's content, the more likely they are to visit your profile and engage with your posts. That's obviously beneficial for your online business.

5. **5. Instagram Stories viewers** (warm/cold): These people are interested in what you have to say, which is why they watch your Instagram Stories. Reach out to them and thank them for supporting you; it'll go a long way.

6. **New Followers** (warm/cold): These prospects have no idea that they're going to purchase something from you. Send them a DM I recommended earlier in this chapter to start a conversation. Use something like: "Hey [name], just wanted to say thanks for the follow. Do you have your own [X business] or are you just enjoying the content?"

7. **On your follower list** (cold): Although these people are on your follower or friends list, it's likely they haven't had any sort of conversation with you in a long time, and

they may have forgotten why they friended or followed you. Reach out to start a conversation. You could say: "Hey [name], just wanted to reach out and say thanks for following me! Hope you're having a great day."

CONVERSATION OPENERS BASED ON SCENARIOS

The next thing you need to understand is how to start conversations based on different scenarios. Let's look at X scenarios and conversation starters for each one.

Application Opener

The goal is to get prospects to expand on what the said in the application because people will only purchase a program when it's associated with a deep enough pain point that *makes* them *want* to change.

Message 1: Hey [name]! I just got your application and I want to say thanks so much for taking the time to fill it out.

Message 2: Noticed in your application that you struggled with [X], can you tell me a bit more about that? I'd love to know more to make sure I can help :)

Instagram Follower

Message 1: Hey [name]! Just wanted to shoot you a message and say thanks so much for the follow!

Message 2: Are you on a [your ideal client] journey or just enjoying the content?

Message 3: What made you decide to hit the follow button?

Engages with Your Content

Message 1: Hey [name], I'm just reaching out and say thanks for all the support on my content.

Message 2: I'm trying to provide more value, so I'm curious what kind of content you want to see more of. Is it fitness, mindset, nutrition or something else?

Message 3: Let me know if you're working on any specific [X goals] at the moment, and if you're struggling to achieve them. I'll do what I can to help you out.

Client Transformation "Likes"

Message 1: Hey [name], I noticed that you're supporting my [client name] transformation and wanted to reach out and say I appreciate that!

Message 2: Let me know if you're working on any specific goals at the moment, and if you're struggling to achieve them. I'll do what I can to give you advice.

Vote on Your Story Polls

Message 1: Hey [name]! I see you! Saw that your biggest struggle is [X thing].

Message 2: I've got a free eBook titled *[Title]*. Mind if I send it your way?

Message 3: Hey [name]! Thanks for the support on my content.

Message 4: Saw that your biggest struggle is [X]. Mind if I ask you a few questions to see if I can help?

Respond Directly to a CTA

Message 1: Hey [name]! Thanks for reaching out and wanting to learn more [CTA].

Message 2: I've got all the details for you here in a minute. First, do you mind if I ask you a few questions to see if I can help you?

DMs are for building relationships. The questions you ask to build relationships can be something like this:

- What's your story? What got you into [nice]? (This one is *gold!)*
- What inspired you to want to get into [industry]?
- When did you know you wanted to be [industry]?
- What made you decide to follow me?
- What resonated most with you about my content?
- What are you currently you doing to get the result you want on your [journey]?
- Where are you located?
- What's the [industry] scene like there?

What do questions like these help us find? They help us find Five-Star Prospects.

I approach DMs through friendly conversation, so I can identify if prospects have any goals they're working toward in the industry I specialize in. As soon as I identify that they have goals they're working on, I transition to the DM script by asking them the magic question: "Mind if I ask you a few questions to see if I can help?"

Once they say "yes," they've given you permission to enter the DM script.

THE DM SCRIPT YOU NEED TO BOOK FIVE TO TEN SALES CALLS A WEEK

You: Mind if I ask you a few questions to see if I can help?

Prospect: They may say something like:

- Sure
- Why not?
- Let's do it
- No problem

You: Awesome! What's the biggest thing you struggle with in your [industry]?

Prospect: It doesn't matter what their response is here; you can move on to the next question.

You: Option 1—I totally get that, I've been through **[mention their struggle]** myself. // Option 2—I've helped a lot of clients with similar situations. (This is how you validate, relate, and lean in.)

You: How long have you been struggling with that?

Prospect: They reply.

You: Oh, I see. So, [mention how long they've been struggling]?

You: Here, you'll relate to what they said with a personal story of a client or yourself. Option 1—I've been through something similar! I struggled to [accomplish X], tried a bunch of different [X solutions], [X fall back]. I get it. // Option 2—

You: What's your No. 1 goal in [industry] right now?

Prospect: They reply.

You: If you got a short answer back, ask an expansive question. Option 1—What do you mean by that? // Option 2—What is your [goal]? // Option 3—Why is [X] important to you?

If you receive a good answer and a good reason why, continue with the DM script. If you receive a decent answer, but not a good reason why, ask them to expand on their why.

Prospect: They reply.

You: You [goal] is super realistic. Why is it important to you?

Prospect: They reply.

You: I love it! Would you like some help?

Prospect: What does that look like? or I'd love some help.

You: I'll tell you what ...

You: Why don't we set up a short, fifteen-minute call? We'll go over your [specific struggle] your [goal], and we'll come up with a gameplan to help you get there.

You: You up for that?

Prospect: They'll likely say:

- Sure
- Absolutely
- Sounds good
- I'd love that
- If they ask *How much does it cost?* You'll say:

You: The call is completely free! It's just to come up with an assessment of what you need and a gameplan for you. No matter what, you'll leave the call with value and an idea of what to do to reach [specific goal]. Does that sound fair?

Validate, Relate, Lean In

You: Cool! Just give me a sec.

You: Send your calendar link here.

You: Go ahead and book in now! Spots fill up quick. Once you're done, let me know what time you picked. Cool?

If they don't book within an hour, comment on one of their Instagram posts. Two hours go by, go into the messaging sequence and like one of their messages. When four hours passes, send them another message that asks, "All good?"

If your prospect doesn't book and it goes into the next day, follow up with a quick video. You can say, "Hey [name]! Good [morning, afternoon, evening] just had some time to get back to you. Go ahead and save your spot in my calendar!" Be sure to share your calendar link again.

CHAPTER 9

Rules and Guidelines for DMs

Here are some rules to follow when sending direct messages to make sure you get the most out of your lead generation efforts.

First, don't send novel-length messages. If you send long messages, you look desperate. You're subconsciously communicating to your prospect that you need them more than they need you.

Write one or two sentences max and then send the message. Your conversation needs to feel organic, not like you're copying and pasting.

Keep your communication loops open, meaning end with a question. You can use questions like:

- Okay?
- Cool?
- Make sense?

Remember that urgency matters. The longer you take to respond to prospects, the less likely they'll be to convert. This is the single most important aspect when it comes direct messaging, especially when you have inbound leads reaching out to you.

Think about it from a psychological standpoint: If I'm interested in buying a vehicle from a dealership, I walk in ready to purchase. Yet, I have to wait seven hours before I speak to someone. If that happens, I'm not going to bother waiting. Instead, I'm going to walk out and find a dealership that's willing to immediately meet my needs.

The goal with direct messages is to move the conversation through the DM script as soon as possible and can capture the emotional state the prospect is in while they are communicating with you.

The longer you take to get back to your leads, the less money you are going to make.

What to Do After Booking the Call?

To set up your calendar system, make sure your calendar link includes these settings:

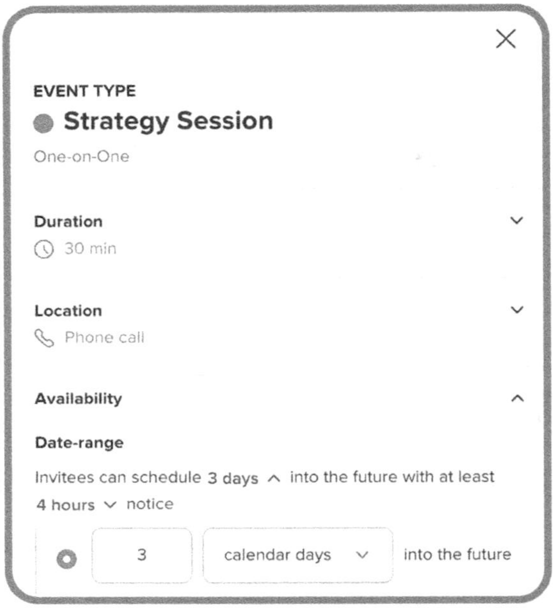

Defaults to a thirty-minute event

You name these calls "Strategy Sessions"

Set questions to collect:

First name
Last name
Phone number
Email address
Instagram username

Then, also ask these questions:

I take my time seriously and commit to showing up ready to give you value. Do you commit to showing up to this call fully present? (YES/NO)

What's your current situation regarding investing in a permanent solution to [X] result?

- Finances aren't an issue. I'm ready to invest.
- My budget is tight, but if the program can guarantee results then I'm interested.
- I don't have the finances to invest in a mentor right now.
- I'm looking for free advice right now.

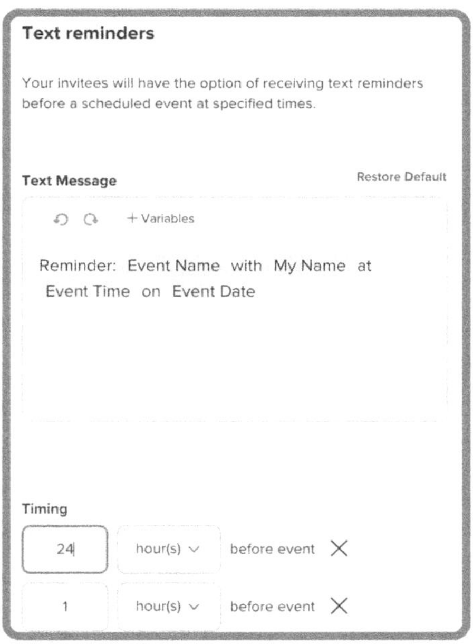

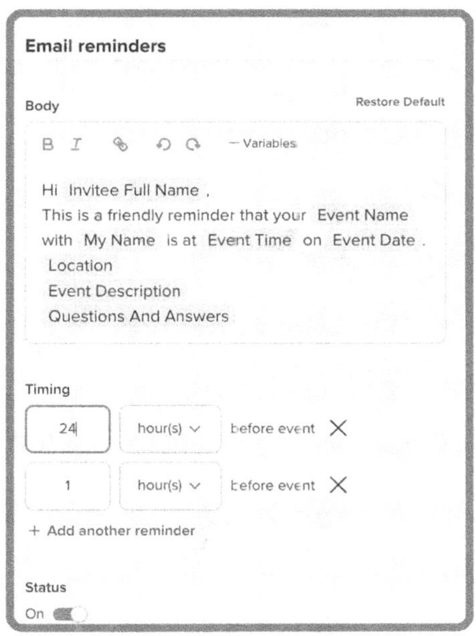

Also set up text and email reminders to go out twenty-four hours before the call and one hour before the call. Last thing regarding settings in your Calendly, make sure the maximum amount of time that someone can book is set to only two days out. The reason for this is you want to capture the prospects emotional state while they are feeling it. If you allow your prospects to book calls three to four days in advance, you're going to run into issues.

Congrats! Your prospect has replied in the chat that they've booked their time slot with you. Now, you're going to want to send some extra free value or resource to get them warmed up before the call. I recommend sending guide you've written and designed that has short, direct, actionable advice that's full of social proof. You could title your guide: *How to [X] Result in [X time] Without Sacrificing [X].*

On page one of your guide, add your story and how you learned the information. Then, structure your guide with three secrets:

> Secret 1: Give value (one-page) and show a testimonial
>
> Secret 2: Give value (one-page) and show a testimonial
>
> Secret 3: Give the value (one-page) and show a testimonial

End the guide with a summary and let prospects know you're going to help them with an actionable plan when you talk.

Here's an example script of how to send that added value document after a prospect has booked time on your calendar:

> **You:** I love it! Let's go! I've got a bonus surprise for you as a thank you for booking.
>
> **You:** Send the guide. (Ahead of time, you'll want to upload the guide to Dropbox, then go use bit.ly to shorten the Dropbox link and turn it into your own custom URL.)

You: This guide will give you a ton of value and help you understand how to get [X] result. Once you're done reading it, come back and let me know what you learned. Cool?

They may read your guide or they don't, it doesn't really matter. If they *do* come back and report a takeaway, make sure you engage with them and let them know you'll give them *more* value on [X subject] on your strategy call.

Every morning, I want you to check your scheduled calendar events for the day. Open your calendar, look at the calls booked, and send each scheduled prospect a video through Instagram direct messsage. You can say:

What's going on [name]? I just checked my calendar and saw we're booked for a thirty-minute call. I'm super excited! We're going to talk about your No. 1 struggle right now in your [X], your No. 1 goal for [X], and I'm going to help you come up with a gameplan to achieve your goals. Bring a pen and paper—it's going to be awesome. I'll chat with you soon!

Your show-up percentages for sales calls will come in at 70 to 90% if you do this.

SUMMARY

In this chapter, we discussed the purpose of direct messages. We also talked about how to start conversations with potential clients. From there, we dove into how to identify whether a prospect is cold, warm, or hot.

You learned what to say to start conversations based on specific scenarios, and I gave you exact scripts for these situations. You also learned where to find leads on Instagram and the order of which to communicate with those leads.

I taught you the Validate, Relate, Lean In strategy to build relationships with prospects during your DM process. I also gave you the *entire* script to book qualified sales calls using your calendar.

Finally, you learned how to handle the pre-call process, so you get the most people to show up for their scheduled calls as possible.

In the next chapter, we'll discuss how to turn prospects into paying clients.

CHAPTER 10

SELLING HIGH TICKET ONLINE PACKAGES

So, you want to sell some sh*t? In this chapter, I'll teach you the entire blueprint I've used to generate more than $30,000,000 in sales in six years.

We are going to dive deep into personal and sales psychology, and I'm also going to give you step-by-step tactics for every part of the sales process. If you don't take action with this information, it's going to be useless. You need to be ready to commit to the work and learn the exact sales processes I've used in my business. If you're ready to do that, then let's dive into the five mindsets of ten-million-dollar salespeople.

1. They have the money and they're going pay you.

Many of you shoot yourself in the foot regarding your sales calls because you convince yourself that the prospect doesn't have any money—before you even get on the call. The problem with that mindset often stems from the fact that you entered entrepreneurship after a typical nine to five job. If you were like me when I first started, I didn't have a lot of money. So, I naturally assumed that other people were in that same position before I got on sales calls.

That thinking, however, is wrong and it will *absolutely* ruin your calls before they start. Understand that the prospect showed up to the call knowing that you have a product or service that you offer. Know that they have a problem they need help solving. As a result of taking a call with you and investing in your program, they could receive a permanent solution for their problem.

With those things in mind, you also need to assume they have the money and they are going to buy from you. Subscribing to this mindset ensures that you show up to your calls with more confidence, and the prospect will sense that from you.

2. Every "No" is one step closer to a "yes."

Listen, I don't care how good you are at sales, you are never going to close 100% of your deals. It doesn't happen. There's not a salesperson on the planet that has a 100% closing rate. The best salespeople can move from rejection to rejection and not lose their enthusiasm. The mindset you need to have is "every 'no' is one step closer to a 'yes.'" This means, when you get a client who decides to join your coaching program, you're absolutely thrilled about that. When someone says "no," to your offer, that's also good. It means you're one step closer to a yes, and it also means that you're going to learn from the specific instance so that the next time you're faced with a similar situation you'll have a different outcome.

3. Either they sell excuses or you sell your program.

This mindset is simple. If your prospect hangs up the phone without taking action, that means you bought their excuses. There's no other way around it. You have legitimate reasons why your prospect needs to join your coaching program, and they have legitimate reasons they can't opt in to your program. They either sell you on the validity of their excuses or you sell them on they need your program.

Many salespeople struggle because they get one rejection and then they instantly fold their cards. You must expect objections from your prospects. If they didn't have objections or excuses, they'd already have the results they want! So, be prepared to counter their excuses and get them to opt in to your program.

4. Intend to serve and the sale will come.

You don't want to come across salesy, but the truth is that when you approach your sales calls with a different perspective—serving not selling—you're going to identify exactly what your prospect is struggling with. You're going to learn how long they've been struggling and how it's impacting their life. Then, you're going to be able to tell them exactly why they need to act now and not later. When you present this information to a prospect, they'll feel stupid turning down your offer.

Show up to your sales calls with the intention to serve. You're not going to have "commission breath," meaning come across desperate for the sale. Enter every sales call with the perspective that you genuinely want to help. When your prospect senses that you genuinely want to help, they'll be more likely to want to work with you in a 1:1 coaching environment.

5. Treat every sales call with respect.

Every person who books a call with you is someone you can help and transform forever. Understand that. Have reverence for that. You're not simply on a sales call, you have an opportunity to improve someone's life. If that person joins your program, they're going to be significantly better off than not being in your program. Treat every single sales call with respect. Show up early and prepared. Dress the part. When you look good, you feel good, and when you feel good, you sell well. Dress like a professional; don't show up in your sweatpants like you don't care. I'm not saying you have wear a suit and tie for your sales calls, but dress like you care and take pride in your work.

I shouldn't have to say this, but *never* bail on a sales call. If you bail, your business and your personal life will lack integrity. Your word is your bond. Show up to every call prepared, ready to serve, ready to help, and ready to change the person's life on the other end of the call.

How to Sell High-Ticket Online Packages

I broke down how to sell high-ticket online packages into an eleven-step process, which may sound like a lot, but it's so simple that my little sister in fifth grade could follow it to sell high-ticket programs. Here are the eleven steps that I'll discuss in detail:

1. Pre-frame
2. Why now, why me
3. Pain points
4. Vision
5. The gap
6. Give advice
7. Test commitment levels
8. Pitch to their problems
9. Get them to sell it back to you
10. Drop the price
11. Overcome objections
12. Secure payment and onboard

1: Pre-frame and Set the Tone

The thirty seconds to two minutes of your sales call will set the tone for your entire call. You're not trying to be their friend. People don't buy from friends; they buy from coaches who they have rapport with. So, how you start your call matters. You need to make sure you position yourself as an authority within two minutes of starting your call. As soon as your prospect joins the call, they are going to wonder "How long is this going to take?" Then, they are going to think, "What are we going to talk about?"

Let's talk about how you're going to address these thoughts within two minutes of the start to your call.

Pre-Frame to Start the Call:

Start the call with energy and enthusiasm. Don't go overboard, and don't be boring. Find the *right* amount of energy for the call. Here's a script:

> **You:** Hey [name]! How's it going?
>
> *Prospect:* Let them reply and engage in small talk).
>
> **You:** How's your day been so far?
>
> *Prospect:* They'll ask you how your day's going as well.
>
> **You:** Awesome! Listen, I've got back-to-back calls booked today. Are you cool if we jump straight into our conversation?

This line will communicate to your prospect that you are in demand, and you have stuff going on. Even if you're *not* in demand (yet), and you don't have stuff going on, still say this. You're instantly going to put yourself in the driver's seat. Once they agree, you are going to say:

> Alright [name], so what we're going to do on today's call is I'm going to ask you a few questions about your [niche] journey. We're going to figure out what your goals are, what you're struggling with, and then I'm going to help you come up with a gameplan to achieve these goals. At the end of the call, if I feel that I can help you out, I'll invite you to work with me. If not, I'll point you in a different direction. Does that sound good?

This script will set the tone for your call and give your prospect a clear picture of what to expect. Let's break down what a pre-frame is. "Pre" means before we get into the call. "Frame" means an agreed upon container between two individuals. I'll give you an example:

You go to the doctor for an earache. The frame is that the doctor is the expert, and you are the person with a problem. You understand that frame when you enter the doctor's office. That's why you don't question what the doctor prescribes, you pick up your medication from the pharmacy.

If you walk into a college class and you see a professor writing on the whiteboard, you understand that the professor is in charge of the class. You understand that when you walked into class, the professor was the expert. You are the student who is expected to show up for class and take tests to receive grades that are based on how well you learned from the expert.

A frame is an agreed upon container between two people. Notice how I said "agreed upon." Framing doesn't unless both people agree to the frame.

On the other hand, however, when you get someone to agree to the frame you've set, you've communicated that you are the authority and your prospect is the client, which also communicates that you're going to coach them.

2: Why Now, Why Me

Unless your prospect feels a sense of urgency, they will delay action. Avoid telling your prospect to decide because they will then resist action, which is called sales resistance. If, however, you can get them to realize, for their own reasons, that they need to take action right then, they will feel more intrinsically motivated to take action.

So, in the next part of the call your goal is to make your prospect aware, through their own words and reasoning, why they need to take immediate action. Start with the next few questions but understand this fundamental concept: Why now and why me are two of the most powerful questions you can ask on a sales call. It pushes your prospect to provide reasons why they need to solve their problem immediately. The two questions also urge your prospect to justify why you're the best option to solve their problem. Do this correctly and your prospect will feel a sense of urgency.

You'll instantly lighten up the tone and mood of your call by transitioning with this question:

> **You:** Alright, tell me a bit about yourself. What's your story? What inspired you to start a [niche] journey?
>
> *Prospect:* They respond.
>
> **You:** Amazing. (Validate, relate, lean in, just like you learned in the direct messaging chapter). What inspired you to reach out to me? (This is a "why me" question.)

The "tell me a bit about your journey. What's your story" questions are important questions. Typically, they will get your prospect to open up more about themselves, which you'll need in order to know if you want to close the deal that day. The "validate, relate, lean in" questions are from the same communication style you used in DMs to book the call in the first place. In simple terms, don't run through the script like a robot—have a conversation.

Here's an example: Your prospect says reason they got into fitness is so they could be a good example for their kids. You can relate because you also have kids. So, you could reply with something like, "I love that you want do this for your kids (this is how you validate). I have two kids myself, so I understand the importance of wanting to lead by example for them (this is how you relate).

Now, you lean in, which means ask the next question in the script.

Also, sidenote. You need to be taking notes during your calls. Every key phrase, like a specific word they use to describe their goals or important details, your prospect says are notes you should be marking in bullet point notes. You'll need those talking points during your pitch, and you'll need to use their words to overcome their objections when and if they come up.

3: Pain Points

During this part of the script, you're going to identify the problems your prospect brought up during the call. So, it's important how you ask the next questions. Do not run through this part of the script like you're desperate; if you do you'll activate your prospect's sales resistance. That will make closing the deal much harder.

Instead, I want you to slow down during this next part of the script. I want you to use a curious tone as you get to the root of their pain points. Why they're on a call with you is one of the single most important questions of a sales call. The reason being, your prospect isn't going to buy your program unless they have a problem they need to immediately solve and can't solve it themselves.

Most people lie to themselves. They delude themselves into believing that they're okay as they are. They're good as they are. Essentially, they hide from themselves how much they're struggling.

Your goal with the questions you ask is to uncover their core pain point. What is the *real* reason they got on a call with you. If you're a business coach, maybe they opened up their Stripe account and realized they're not making anywhere close to the type of money they should make. Maybe they realized they hate their job and need to change career paths.

If you're a relationship coach, maybe your prospect is on the verge of a breakup with their spouse, and even though they love their partner dearly they can't seem to find a way to communicate or get on the same page with each other.

If you're a content coach, maybe your prospect has posted for two years without seeing real traction, so they know they have a content quality problem. They're so frustrated and burnt out with trying, however, that they're contemplating giving up.

Whatever their *real* core pain point is—you need to find it.

Pain Points: Approach with Curiosity

> **You:** What's been your biggest struggle when it comes to your [specific] journey?
>
> *Prospect:* If they don't know what they struggle with, you can offer suggestions like most of my best clients struggled with [X, Y, or Z], which one is it for you?
>
> **You:** Makes sense. Can you tell me a bit more about that?
>
> *Prospect:* They answer.
>
> **You:** Fair enough. How long has that been an issue for you?
>
> *Prospect:* They answer.

You: Wow, that's a long time to struggle with [X]. How has that impacted your [industry] journey?

Prospect: They answer.

You: Makes sense. Is that something you want to change today or are you happy with how things are going?

You: Okay just so I understand you clearly, [X and Y] are your struggles. It's been happening for [X] time, and you're ready to make a change. Did I miss anything you'd like to discuss or does that sound right? (Summarize their pain points now before your transition to the next step. Doing so will show them you're paying attention.)

As your prospect answers questions, you need to be taking bullet-point notes. That will make it easier to repeat back to your prospect what they said as you summarize. Repeating back what they say is an essential part of communication. It shows you're paying attention. Your prospect will appreciate that and feel understood.

The goal of your call is to make your prospect feel like you understand their problems better than they understand their own problems, which is what will push them to get your help.

4. Vision and Goals

By this part of the call, you have your prospect in their feels. They are beginning to understand that they are not where they want to be, and they're feeling the pain of not being where they want to be. That's a good thing. Pain is a motivating factor. How many times can you think back to a time when you had a major transformation that came on the back end of pain.

Great things come after pain, so you need to make your prospect aware of the pain they're feeling by asking the right questions and getting them to thoroughly consider their situation. This is only *half* the work of what you need in order to sell your prospect a high-ticket online program. The other half you need is a clear goal, a goal to be reached, and a reason to reach that goal. Without that, you'll only make your prospect feel hopeless and in pain. People who are hopeless and in pain don't buy from you.

People who are excited about transitioning from their situation into a new situation are the people who buy from you. They will definitely buy from you if they believe that what they purchase from you will move them from their current state to where they want to be.

Here's the thing about vision and goals, most of your prospects have never *actually* imagined what their life would look like if their problem was completely solved.

Many of your prospects have been in pain for a long time and they've learned how to cope. That's an issue for you for two reasons: One, they don't even know what the problem would look like if it were fully solved. Two, they may not believe in themselves, or in your, to permanently solve their problem.

That's your goal for the next part of your call. You're going to help your prospect get clear on their goal, their vision, and their dream of having their problem completely solved. To help your prospect believe in themselves, you must show them that you believe in them.

You also need to demonstrate to your prospect that you have the solution to their problem, and you can help them permanently solve it. That will help them believe in you.

Vision, Goals, and Primary Motivation

After discussing pain points, I want you to transition to a lighter, more enthusiastic tone.

> **You:** Alright enough of that! Let's talk about your goals. What would you say is your No. 1 goal in [X] industry right now?

Prospect: They respond.

You: Amazing. Why is that [X] goal important to you?

Prospect: They respond.

You: I love that! I believe in you, and I know you can make that happen. How would it make you feel if you hit that goal?

Prospect: They respond.

You: Hell yes! What would change in your life if we made that happen?

Prospect: They respond.

You: Sounds like the dream. What are you doing right now to work toward your goal and make it a reality?

Prospect: They respond.

You: Fair enough. Why is it important for you to make a change now and not later? You could put this off for another two to five years. Why do you want to solve this problem now? (Let them know that all their goals are realistic and attainable with the right plan.)

Now you're going to transition into identifying the gap between where they currently stand and where they want to be.

5. Identifying the Gap

The gap is the distance between where they currently stand and where they want to end up. The gap is also the main reason they would purchase your program. Your prospect believes your program will take them from their current state to where they want to be in the future.

The questions in this section are designed to widen the gap, which essentially means you're going to create *more* distance between where they are and where they want to end up. This will push your prospect to feel an internal sense of urgency to close that gap.

How are they going to close the gap? By working with you.

Identify and Widen the Gap

> **You:** Now that I know what you want, why do you think you haven't been able to achieve these goals on your own?
>
> *Prospect:* They respond.
>
> **You:** Let me play devil's advocate for a moment. Pretend you get off this call and do absolutely nothing. You stay in the same place and for the next year. Maybe it's two more years or five more years that you remain in place. If you don't make progress in [specific area], how would that make you feel?

You *must* ask that last question. You can't be the nice guy or girl and avoid asking it. You *need* to force your prospect to imagine what will happen if they get off the phone and do absolutely nothing.

If you don't convince your prospect to take action or inspire them to work with you during the phone call, there is a high likelihood they'll continue to face challenges for the next few years.

Prospects either ignore their issues or believe they won't be affected by them. Most dislike imagining worst-case scenarios.

Their response to your question may be something like "I'd hate that," or "I refuse to let that happen."

That's when you engage them.

6. Give Advice

Now you're going to deliver value. So, you'll demonstrate your expertise in this part of the script. It's also time to deliver on the promise you made when you messaged with them and in the pre-frame of your call. You say, "I'll help you come up with a gameplan for your specific goals."

You're not going to hold back. Spend two to five minutes diagnosing their problem and providing expert information on exactly how to solve their problem.

Once they recognize their problem and see the solution's viability, you'll discuss the cost of providing permanent support to help them achieve their vision or goal.

Give Value

> **You:** Okay, based on everything you've told me so far, here's exactly how to solve [X] problem. (Don't hold back. I want you to give as much value as you can.)

Here's an example of what you might say:

> "First things first [name], you're eating out three times a week. That's obviously a problem. Since you don't know your actual caloric intake, it's going to make it impossible for you to lose weight. I'm not saying you can never eat out, but when you do eat out you need to make sure you know the exact macros of the foods that you choose.

"Second. You're working out five times a week, which is too much for your fat-loss goals. Not to mention you're doing way too much cardio. Essentially, you're trying to out train your bad diet, but that never works. So, I want you to decrease your workouts and cardio frequency, and I want you to make sure you're focusing on progressive overload.

"Finally, let's talk about your mindset. Multiple times on this call, you've told me "everyone in my family struggles with their weight, that's why it's an issue for me." You need to decide if that's going to be the story you pass down to your kids or if you're going to make an actual change.

"Does that make sense?

"Can you see how if we made these changes how you'd start seeing incredible progress?"

During the give value section of the call, I like to highlight everything my prospect is doing wrong and then talk about how we're going to solve the problem.

I don't say, "this is exactly how you calculate your calories," but I make them aware of their biggest concern if they don't solve their problem. I also address the biggest pain points they brought up already, as well as what I believe are their biggest limiting factors for why they haven't been able to achieve success.

When you can show that you understand their problems better than they understand do, and you have the solution to those problems, they will want to work with you.

7. Test Commitment Levels

You'll be able to identify if your prospect will object to your program based off testing their commitment level. Instead of directly asking, "do you want to pay me to coach you," you're going to use a gauge and a scale to determine how ready your client is to act.

If they are less than the commitment level you need to properly serve them, you're going to challenge them. If your prospect doesn't commit during this stage of call, the chances of them converting and becoming a good client are slim.

There are ways to ask your questions that get your prospect to join your program. If, however, you convince your prospect to join the program but if they're not fully convinced of you, your program, your offer, the timing, or the investment, then you're going to experience a lot of refunds, chargebacks, and disputes. So, it's not worth convincing someone to join your program if their commitment level is too low.

The best way to sell high-ticket online packages is to get people to commit to their own goals. So, the next part of this script involves testing your prospect's commitment levels. If they display a lower commitment level, you're going to challenge it.

Doing so may bring up an underlying objection your prospect has. If that happens, you'll have to be prepared to deal with the objection, re-frame it, overcome it, and re-ask the commitment testing question.

Testing Commitment Levels

> **You:** My program comes with guaranteed results coaching and because of that, I only take on serious people. On a scale of one to ten, with one being "I don't really care about this at all right now," and ten being "I'll do whatever it takes to achieve my goals," how important is it for you to achieve your [X] goal right now?
>
> *Prospect:* They reply with a number. (If your prospect give you any number less than eight, you need to challenge them.)

You: Seven! Damn. That's shocking based on the call we've had so far. You told me [X, Y, and Z] pain and that you've been struggling with it for [X] years. Why are you at a seven?

Prospect: They reply. (They'll likely give you an objection. Something like, "I just want to make sure it fits my budget.")

If that happens:

You: I completely get that, but I didn't ask about your financial situation. I asked about your commitment to your own goals. If I give you a program, are you going to do your very best to follow the program, and get [X] result or are you going to slack off and be lazy?

Prospect: They reply. (They'll likely say "No I'll follow it to the best of my ability.")

You: OK perfect. So, are you a seven or a ten? (If they say anything 8 or higher, you can work with that.)

You: Sounds to me like you're committed to getting [X] result. At the start of the call, I told you I'd let you know if I could help you. The good news is, you're definitely the type of person I can help. Would you like to hear a bit more information about how the program works?

If you skip the commitment level question or you don't challenge them on their low commitment level, then you're going to walk head-first into their objection at the end of the call. A low commitment level is an early indicator that you're going to get an objection at the end of the call. So it's extremely important that you challenge their commitment level during this stage of the script and get them to commit to a higher number than their original one. This micro-commitment strategy will push them to be more convinced that it's the right time, you're the right coach, and they're ready to act.

Once you get your prospect to pass the commitment test, you need to add your qualifier statement. This signals to your prospect that you're about to pitch them and you get them to confirm that they are OK with that. Once they agree, you set the frame and you can price present.

8. Pitch to Their Problems

The program presentation is where most salespeople mess up. They overexplain program features and benefits and prospects get bored. If you don't want that to happen to you, follow my formula to present your offer.

First, you need to know that we don't think in words, we think in pictures. We use words to communicate, but those words create images in our minds.

For example, when I mention "tiger," what happened when you read the word? You saw a picture of a tiger in your mind, right? You didn't think about the word "tiger," you thought about a giant animal that lives in the forest.

So, I keep this in mind when I get to price presenting. I explain my product in a way that creates a visual for my prospect, which gives them something they can tangibly grip onto. This is especially important if you're selling something intangible, such as relationship coaching, mindset coaching, or any service that doesn't have a direct, physical result. You must create a visual for your program breakdown, so you provide your prospect something they can grasp.

To be successful, you'll need to identify three to four pillars of your service and you're going to present those pillars using a diagram that you'll have your prospect draw.

Break your niche into four or five categories.

- If you're a content coach, these pillars may be: research, scripting, filming, editing, and posting.
- If you're a fitness coach, maybe your pillars are: mindset, nutrition, exercise, and accountability.
- As a business coach, your pillars may be: attracting clients, converting clients, delivering a service, and scaling a business.
- If you're a relationship coach, your pillars could be: relationship with self, relationship with others, and relationship with God.
- If you're a sales coach, pillars could look like: mindset, sales psychology, in-field sales training, and overcoming objections.

Next, you'll use those pillars to describe your coaching offer in a way that's easy for your prospect to understand.

You're not going to sell the features and benefits of your program. You are going to sell the transformation from your prospect's current state to where they want to end up. To do that effectively, you will use the pain points your prospect told you about at the start of the call. When you explain your product or service, you will use keywords they used to sell them your offer. You're also going to have your prospect draw a visual representation of your offer as you speak.

Program Breakdown

Here's an example script using business coach pillars:

> **You:** Grab a pen and piece of paper [name]? Do me a favor now and write down [X] at the top of the piece of paper because that's our goal. Next, I want you to draw a triangle in the middle of the piece of paper. (Pause.) Got it? Okay great. At the top of

your triangle, I want you to write down the word attract (explain). Following along so far?

Prospect: Yes.

You: Perfect. In the bottom right point of the triangle, I want you to write convert (explain). Does this make sense?

Prospect: Yes.

You: Awesome. In the bottom left, write deliver (explain). Make sense?

Prospect: Yes.

You: In the middle of the triangle, write scale (explain). Is this all making sense so far?

Prospect: Yes.

Okay perfect. What part of the program feels like it would benefit you the most?

Prospect: They reply. (They'll sell themselves to you.)

You: Why do you think [X] would benefit you the most?

Prospect: They reply.

You: Perfect, now let's get into the logistics.

You want to make your prospect understand the overarching theory behind what you're doing. That's why you make them draw a diagram. Doing so gives them something tangible to look at. When your prospect sits there with a physical roadmap (the diagram) to reach their goals, they're going to be more receptive to the game plan you present to get them to their desired results.

10: Drop the Price

You're not selling features, you're selling transformation, but you do need to touch on the features. If you have an overarching theory without a roadmap to get there, then the prospect is not going to feel confident in your ability to deliver on the promise. Here's the hard thing with the high-ticket space: There's a lot of garbage. Some people are good at marketing and selling but their client results are decent—at best. So, the market as a whole doesn't trust *you*.

With the theory we've discussed in this chapter, and the way you show up on social media, the likelihood of you closing a prospect significantly increases, especially if you follow my plan. When you get to the point where you're going to drop the price, you want to be brief with your explanations and walk your prospect through the *actual* deliverables of your program. Do a short summary of what's included in the program. At this point in the call, your prospect should already be sold on you. They're wondering what the plan will be to get them from their current place to where they want to be.

My coaching program includes twenty-four-hour support, three live calls a week, and a step-by-step, guaranteed results blueprint. Here's how it works:

> **The Course:** You receive a step-by-step blueprint to get [result]
>
> **Coaching Calls**: We'll talk three times a week in live coaching calls where you can ask any questions and we make sure you're getting [X] result.
>
> **Community**: You get access to six months of coaching and support with unlimited questions

and I'll answer any and all questions within twenty-four hours.

Does this all make sense so far? Perfect.

The program is six months long, and there are two options to enroll. Option one, which is our most popular option and will save you one thousand dollars, is five thousand dollars. Option two, is a bit easier on your cash flow and it's one thousand dollars a month. Out of those two options, which one works best for you? Then, you need to pause. Let them process.

Most online coaches mess up here because as soon as they drop the price, they get weird and allow their own money mindset issues to creep in. So, they start overexplaining and the prospect doesn't have time to think, so they end up rejecting the program.

Give your prospect an alternate close at the end. Then allow them to process and decide. If high ticket sales was easy and everyone said "yes," then I wouldn't need to be a business coach. You could follow the script, get sales, and be done with it. Unfortunately, it's not that easy. More than likely, you'll experience objections—that's human nature. Everyone has excuses. If they didn't, they'd already have results.

11: Overcoming Objections

The best time to overcome objections is before they come up. It's why you have your Calendly questions set up to ask the budget question. It's why you test their commitment level. It's also why you need to be paying attention for red flags on the call. Red flags can sound like:

- Asking about the price during the call
- Mentioning their spouse during the call
- Talking about starting in a few months during the call

If your prospect asks about the price of your program during the call, it's a potential red flag that they can't afford it. If that happens, you can say, "I have a program that suits all budgets, but let's make sure I can even help you before we discuss price. I want to ask you a few questions. Sound good?"

If they *do* bring up price during the call, you need to get a feel of their spending habits without being invasive. Ask them if they go out, if they drink, or if they smoke because all those things at the end of the call can be used as examples regarding the ways they're currently wasting money.

Ask them how much money they've spent on finding a solution, including supplements, therapy, other coaches, etc. That information can be used when you properly share your guarantee.

If they bring up their spouse during the call, here's an easy, two question series to get them to eliminate the spouse objection. "Oh, you have a significant other? That's awesome. Does [he/she] know we're speaking today?" If they respond "yes," you can reply with, "[He/she] does? That's amazing. And typically speaking, is [he/she] supportive of your [X] journey?" The prospect responds that their partner is supportive. So, you can say, "[He/She] wants you to be happy?" Your prospect will always say "yes" to that question. If the spouse objection comes up later, you've already pre-handled it.

If the prospect wants to push off their program start date during the call, that's a red flag and you'll need to stress the importance of starting now up to four times throughout the call. You can say, "You've been struggling with this for two years? Damn, that's a long time! What has shifted to make this a "right now" problem you want to solve? Why not put it off a few more years?"

You're going to experience objections no matter what. If it were easy to pre-handle them all and never have objections, I wouldn't have a job. So, here's how to handle four main objections, which are time, money, spouse, and "I need to think about it."

I Need to Think About It

There's always a reason underneath this objection, it can be budget, time, spouse, or just that it's a big decision and they need to process it. But the "I need to think about it," response is a generic and broad answer. You must always get further clarification from the prospect. Here's how:

> *Prospect:* I need to think about it.
>
> **You:** I totally understand, thanks for being honest with me. And just so I'm clear, what exactly is it that you need to think about? (You can ask this question in pleasant, curious tone.)

Your question will often reveal their main objection, which will likely be, "well I just have to check the budget or I need to talk to my wife, etc."

When you ask, "What exactly is it that you need to think about," you'll quickly unlock their real objection and be able to move to the objection framework.

The *only* exception to this rule is if they say "It's just a really big decision and I need to process decisions like this before I take action." Here's how you handle that.

Big Decision "Think About It" Objection

> **You:** Okay that makes sense [name]. To be super clear, big decision aside, does this program sound like what you're looking for? Is there anything about the program you don't like? Or do you really feel like it's going to help you reach the [X] goal you mentioned and it's just a big decision?

If your prospect mentions anything about the program they don't like, then you'll have to sell them on why that part of the program will help them reach their goals.

If they say the program sounds like what they're looking for and they don't bring up anything about they do not like, here's where you can go a layer deeper.

> **You:** Listen, I totally get it's a big decision and thank you so much for being honest with me. You remind me of my client [name]. He signed up a few weeks ago and made a big decision to invest in this coaching program and now he has [X] result. He's the happiest he's ever been. Now let me ask you [name], if all we did was get you [X] result that we talked about on this coaching call today, would that investment be worth it?
>
> *Prospect:* They're going to agree and tell you the investment would indeed be worth it.
>
> **You:** Well listen, I know it's a big decision, so let me remove the risk for you. If you make the decision to join today, we work together for the next six months and you don't get the [X] result we talked about on this call, I'll send you a full refund of every dollar you paid. The worst case scenario is I suck, but you at least learn some valuable information that you can use for the rest of your life, and you get a refund. The best case scenario is we celebrate because you hit [X] result in your journey and you're the happiest you've ever been. How does that sound?

That is called a conditional money-back guarantee and you can use it to push people over the edge when they're standing at the edge but thinking about it. That money-back guarantee can push them over the edge and get them to commit to their goals.

That being said, they still may bring up one another objection, time, money, spouse, after that. If so, follow the objection framework listed below.

Time, Money, or Spouse Objections

When a prospect says, "I need to check with my [wife/husband]," or "I need to check my budget," or "I want to start next week," you must isolate the objection. Make sure that it's the only reason your prospect isn't taking action. If you do not isolate their objection, they may conceal the *actual* reason why they don't want to move forward. Even if you do successfully remove the smokescreen, you're still going to get smacked in the face with another objection. So, no matter what the objection is, follow this two-step framework:

Overcome Objections

> **You:** Okay that makes sense [name]. To be super clear, [objection] aside, does this program sound like what you're looking for? Is there anything about the program you don't like? Or do you feel like it's going to help you reach [X] goal you mentioned and we just need to deal with [X] objection?

The two questions above will push your prospect to reveal anything about the program that they may feel uncertain around. Then, you can have a conversation with them and help them see the value.

If your prospect says, "No, the program does sound amazing, I just need to [X] objection." Then, you can move to the objection framework in this chapter.

> *Prospect:* I need to check my budget.

> **You:** Perfect and thank you for being honest with me. So, the five thousand dollars for six months is a little but too much. Is that correct?

> *Prospect:* Yes.

> **You:** Okay, so is it that you don't have a credit card you can put it on, savings, or something else?

We want to get them to think resourcefully about ways they can come up with the payment to be able to act that day.

If they say they *do* have a credit card or savings, they can use.

> **You:** I love it. And listen, [name], my goal is to help you get [X] thing. (We need to get them into results based thinking instead of cost based thinking). So, at the end of our six months working together, if all we did was get you [X] thing and you felt the best you've ever felt in your life, would the investment be worth it?
>
> *Prospect:* They say "yes."
>
> **You:** Perfect. Sounds like you're ready to get started. Would you prefer to do the paid in full option and save some money, or pay monthly?

If they say they don't have a credit card, savings, anything to use to pay, here's what you say:

> **You:** Tell you what [name], why don't we do this. Let's get you started at the one thousand dollars a month program. That's a lot easier on the wallet, and we're going to make sure we get you [X] goal and we start seeing progress and results right away. And, I'm so confident that you're going to get [X] result that if you follow my direction and advice and you still haven't received the result you want at the end of six months, I'll send you a full refund of everything you've paid. Does that sound good?

Just like that, you overcame the money objection and collected some cash.

Spouse Objection

Here's my perspective, getting a prospect to fully commit without talking to their spouse is a recipe for buyer's remorse and chargebacks. That's why this objection is best overcame at the start of the call by asking if their spouse is on board and supports them and their goals. If you do get the spouse objection, the first thing you need to do is understand the prospect.

Here's a script you can use:

> **You:** (After you isolate their objection) Totally understand that you need to speak to your partner. I have a spouse who I run all my major decisions by as well. Does your spouse know we are speaking today?
>
> *Prospect:* Yes
>
> **You:** Okay perfect. And typically speaking are they supportive of your goals? Like they want you to be happy?

This is going to help the prospect realize that their spouse is indeed on board and wants them to win, which will help us solidify a deal on the call or at least get some sort of financial commitment.

> **You:** I'll tell you what, I understand you need to speak to your spouse and I respect that decision. I've also been on hundreds of these calls, and I know for a fact that if you get off this call and don't take any sort of action then the likelihood that you come back and start getting [X] result is one in ten. So, let's do this, talk to your spouse and make sure

> this decision makes sense. Let's do a one hundred dollar deposit. This deposit is completely refundable, so if you talk to your spouse and [he/she] says I suck or they aren't interested in you getting [X] result then I'll send you a full refund. I just want to see that you are ready to act on your own goals. Does that sound fair enough?

I've closed more than thirty million dollars in sales and in my experience if I get a financial commitment outside of a refundable deposit then I experience more chargebacks, disputes and refunds.

Are there talking tracks you can use to get someone completely off the fence without talking to their spouse? Absolutely.

Why don't I teach them?

Because I don't want to set you up for chargebacks, disputes and refunds.

Now this will do one of two things.

1) They agree, and give you a deposit, in which case you'll collect the cash on the spot.

> **You:** Okay perfect, so how much time do you need to speak with your spouse?

They'll give you a timeframe and then you'll say, "how about I give you a shout in [X timeframe] from now?"

Your prospect may also say "tomorrow," and your reply would be, "Okay great, how about we do a call tomorrow at the same time to keep things easy for us?"

2) They object and say they still need to speak to their spouse before putting down any sort of financial commitment.

If this is the case, you need to lean out. If you keep leaning in to overcome the objection, they're going to get pushy vibes and won't be willing to have a follow up conversation with you. So you'll say:

> **You:** Okay. I totally get it; thanks for being honest with me. How much time do you need to speak with your spouse to make sure that [X] result is what you want and that this is going to be a good decision for you?

They'll give you a timeframe for them to speak to their spouse, and then you'll say "Perfect, how about I give you a shout in [X timeframe] and then we can go from there, fair enough?"

They'll agree, and you can say, "Awesome. And just so I'm clear before we go, if your spouse did have an objection to you getting started today, what do you think that objection would be? Just so I know what questions you may have when we speak again."

That question is going to give you the ability to cement the results you are going to get and help the prospect get the right things to say to their spouse to ensure the spouse is on board.

Their response will also often reveal the real objection to the program if the prospect was simply using their spouse as a smokescreen. Use discretion. Sometimes, you can sit there on the spot and close that client. Sometimes, you need to lean out and wait for the next call.

I Want to Start Later Objection

Oftentimes, the "I want to start later" objection can solved by asking "Why now and why me" questions throughout the script. You want to make sure your prospect feels the urgency to take action at that moment to solve their problem based off of their internal reasonings.

Here's a script you can follow:

> **You:** (After isolating their objection) Perfect. So why do you want to start later?
>
> *Prospect:* Typically, their response will be about budget.

> *You:* Okay perfect. So, you don't have a credit card you can put it on, savings you can use, or something else?

At this point, there are times when the prospect realizes they have a credit card or savings they could put it on and you seal the deal.

There are also times where the prospect does have the money and it's not a concern, but they're going away on vacation or they're spending their money another way.

In this cast, you must close on that call. If your prospect loses the emotion they're feeling as they consider signing up for your coaching program, they are gone!

So, here's how you handle that:

> **You:** Alright [name], I totally get that you're doing [X] and you want to be fully focused when you get started. I've been on hundreds of these calls and I know for a fact that if you hang up without taking any action the likelihood that you fully commit to your goals and get [X] result drops to a one in ten chance.
>
> So, you like the program and I like you. You know for a fact this is going to work, so let's get the investment taken care of today. That way we can remove all the logistics when you get back from your vacation on [X date] and we can hit the ground running and start seeing progress right away.
>
> I'll also send you a guide to getting started in the meantime. So, while you're on vacation you at least have a bit of an idea of what we're working on while you're away. Does that sound good?

If, however, a prospect says, "I don't have it in my budget to pay for this right now, but I want to start [X timeframe]! Then, you *must* get some sort of financial commitment from them.

If they hang up the phone without giving you cash, the likelihood of closing that prospect drops to a one in ten chance. We don't want that; we want money on the phone. So, you can say:

> **You:** Okay that makes sense! Well I'll tell you what [name], I'm super committed to you getting [X] result, and I know for a fact we can make that happen. I've also been on hundreds of these calls and I know if you hang up without taking any action, there's a high chance that nothing changes. So here's what I can do. Let's get you started next week, and let's do a one-hundred-dollar deposit to secure your spot in the program right now. That way, when we get started next week, I'll already have your program done and we can get off to the races. Does that sound good?

What About "Follow Up" Calls?

I don't care how good you are or how much you follow these scripts—sales is a numbers game. Sometimes, even though you're cool, smart, talented, and look good people still won't convert on a sales call.

For that reason, you need to understand when to lean out and book a follow up call. Here's my rule: I always push 10% more then I'm comfortable with on sales calls to get used to the idea of overcoming objections.

So, if you always accept the first "no," then push for the second "no." If you always accept the second "no," then push for the third one. Finally, I'd end at the third "no" because at that point the prospect is going to get pushy vibes. Once you feel that you've done everything in your power to close the prospect and it's still a "no," here's how you handle that.

When to Book a Follow Up Call

> **You:** Alright [name], I can tell you need a bit of time to process [X objection] and make the right decision for you and your [X] journey. I think we should book a follow up call, so I give you some time to consider and make sure it's the right move for you. How much time do you need? Do you have some time later today or tomorrow?

Asking the question that way will add some urgency, but they may say they need a day or two.

At which point, you can say, "Amazing. How about we book for the exact same time on [X] day to make it easy?"

The "same time" strategy removes all resistance from booking follow up calls with your prospects and makes it easy to do. If that time doesn't work, suggest an hour earlier or an hour later.

The last thirty seconds of your call is the only part your prospect is going to remember. So, at the end of every call, you have to know how you left the call. The *only* option is to leave it on a high note. Once you book the follow up call and you've got a time locked on the calendar, you're going to say:

You: Alright [name], listen I'm extremely confident that I'm going to be able to help you get [X] result and I'm looking forward to being a part of your journey and helping you with this. While I'm here, are there any final questions you have for me regarding [X]? Is there anything I can do to help you right now?

Answer any question they have, then finish with "I hope you have the best day of your entire life. I'll send you a few free resources before we speak next and I'll also send you a few client transformations that have similar stories as you. That way, you can see the results of us working together. I'm looking forward to our next call."

That script will get your follow-up call booked and set up for massive success.

12: Securing Payment

If you were able to overcome the objections the prospect gave you on the call and you got them to the closing table, great! I'm going to teach you how to collect payment on the spot.

Once your prospect agrees to act, you're on the one-yard line. You don't score the touchdown until the ball is in the end zone. I don't want you to spend all of your time and energy getting your prospect to the point where they agree that they want to take action and then you don't secure a commitment from them on the phone.

I used to do that all the time. After my prospect said "yes" and agreed to pay me, I spent the next five to eight hours staring at my phone and anxiously awaiting for the prospect to follow through on their commitment.

Here's what I started doing that massively increased the amount of cash I collected on the phone. As a result, it skyrocketed the amount of money my business made. I started collecting cash on the spot.

To effectively collect payment on the phone, you need to have your payment links already set up.

So, if you're selling a five thousand dollar offer or a nine hundred dollar offer, all your payment links need to be ready before you get on the call.

That way, when someone gives you a "yes," you have a payment link ready to go.

Here's a script you can use to secure your payment:

> **You:** Okay perfect [name]. I'm sending you a text. Let me know when you receive it. (The text you send is the payment link, but you don't say that. You just ask if they received the text.)
>
> *Prospect:* Yes, I received it.
>
> **You:** Perfect. Go ahead and get that taken care of right now for me. It only takes about thirty

> seconds. In the meantime, I'm going to get all of your onboarding documents ready. Once you're all done, I'm going to walk you through onboarding and get you taken care of. Cool?

They might ask, "Do I have to take care of this right now?" To which you will reply, Yep! It only takes about thirty seconds."

They will realize you're not going anywhere. So, they'll get their wallet, find their credit card, and pay you.

When I first started doing this step with my own business, it was awkward that I would mute the phone on my end once I told them what I needed them to do. I would not let myself say anything.

You can do the same because you told them that you were going to get their onboarding documents ready.

If a few minutes tick by and they're fumbling, you can make light of the situation with a joke and ask "How are we doing over there?"

They'll come back to the phone and say, "All taken care of."

You just closed a paid in full high-ticket client.

Here's what you must do next. You have to ask them how they are feeling and then validate their emotions. They may feel anxious or they may feel overwhelmed. The last thing you would want is for them to get off the call feeling those emotions without processing them with you on the call. That's a recipe for buyer's remorse.

Secure the sale by cementing the payment and affirming their decision. Then give them a very clear picture of what will happen next.

Onboarding and Securing the Sale

Here's a script you can use:

> **You: [name]**, wow are you feeling? Nervous? Excited? Ready?

Prospect: They reply. (No matter what they say, you'll move on.)

You: I totally get it. You just made a huge decision to transform your life and it's going to be the best decision you've ever made. [X emotion] is completely normal to feel; it just means you're about to go through a massive transformation and that's exciting.

Prospect: They reply.

You: Okay perfect so what we're going to do next is I'm going to send you over a welcome email. Inside of the email, you'll see the client agreement, which basically outlines what I expect from you as a client and what you can expect from me as a coach. Beyond that, you'll see a link to join the community. That's where you're going to get access to [X] community full of other members who are doing amazing things. As soon as you join, I want you to introduce yourself and tell everyone what your goals are. Finally, [X] link is going to be in that email as well. I want you to create an account and get yourself all set up. You should see the email in your inbox now. Did you get it?

Prospect: They reply "yes."

You: Perfect. Do me a favor and complete that homework right after this call. All I want you to do is reply "done" to the email once you completed everything. Cool?

Just like that, you'll successfully onboard a client into your high-ticket online coaching offer.

There are many levels in terms of successfully onboarding, however, this serves as a fundamental baseline.

If your business is small, you could do a one-on-one kick off call. If your business is bigger, you could do a group kick off call.

SUMMARY

We broke down how to convert high-ticket clients on the phone. I gave you my entire sales process to convert interested prospects into paying clients, and I walked you through my twelve-part sales process. Plus, I gave you a script that you can use immediately upon the completion of this book.

You learned how to overcome the four main objections—time, money, spouse, and I need to think about it—and you now have the framework you can use on every sales call going forward. Finally, at the end of this chapter you learned how to close the deal, secure payment on the phone, and successfully onboard the client.

THE FULL PHONE SCRIPT

CHAPTER 11

SCALING YOUR BUSINESS AND ADDING FUEL TO THE FIRE

Let's talk about how to add some fuel to the fire that is your business, so you can scale it and take it to the next level. This chapter is for you if you're clearing $10,000 or more a month in your business. Buckle up, let's talk about scaling this business.

To do so, we're going to go back in time to when my business coaching made me $30,000 a month. At that time, I went to a business coaching conference. I sat in the audience and listened to a guy, we'll call him John, talk about his fascinating business model and how he had eight virtual assistants (Vas) working for him full time. They worked all day, every day to book qualified prospects for sales calls through John's Instagram account.

"All I have to do is post content," John said, "and my VAs generate my leads."

I thought it was genius. I pulled John aside afterward, and I spoke to him about scaling my online business to $100,000 a month. He agreed to a Zoom call so I could pick his brain. I learned information on that call with John that completely changed the trajectory of my business—and my life.

I currently have a team of VAs who work for me. My Instagram account has full coverage from five in the morning until midnight every day. The sole responsibility my VAs have is to book calls with people who are interested in learning more about my coaching. With this system, we book more than three hundres sales calls a month from my Instagram and we generate three hundred sell-by-chat opportunities. I've also taught this system to some of most successful, best-selling-authors in the industry.

What is a Virtual Assistant (VA)?

A VA is plugged into your Instagram account and helps you manage your inbox, reply to comments, and book qualified sales calls to your calendar for you.

The reason I want you to make $10,000 or more a month before you consider hiring a VA is because there is there a financial aspect associated with hiring a VA, and there's also a skills cost. You must have the necessary skill set to train your VA to book qualified sales calls for you. If you don't, your VA won't be much help and you'll burn through leads.

So how do you develop the necessary skill set to train a VA? You get your business to $10,000 a month. At that financial level, you clearly have a baseline understanding of how to book calls through DMs, otherwise you wouldn't be at that income level.

Let's get into the logistics of having someone speak *for* you through your Instagram account. At first, it's weird. So, you need to not only hire the right person, but you also need to have standards and procedures in place for how your VA will in your account.

How much do you pay a VA?

In my business, I pay a base rate of four dollars an hour plus a 5% commission on cash collected for all new cash sales. This equals $650 base salary plus the 5% commission.

I get affordable VAs overseas. Are there Canadian and American VAs you can hire? Sure. In my opinion, however, they're overpriced and they don't work half as hard as someone from Honduras, Mexico, or the Philippines.

CHAPTER 11

Two Ways to Hire VAs

There are two ways to hire a VA. The first is you pay an agency to find, hire, and train a VA for you. I will say that there are a lot of subpar VA agencies that charge $10,000 to $15,000 to place a VA and they over promise and then the VA under delivers. If you're going to hire a VA, and you want a good one, and you want to pay an agency that's good at what they do, reach out to Magnus VA.

The second way to hire a VA is to search Facebook groups for candidates or create a job posting for your open VA position. If you use Facebook groups or job sites, you'll need to follow the following step-by-step formula to find and hire your VA.

Where to Find VAs

- Starting Salary:
  - $650 USD monthly base pay
  - Plus 2% commission from new sales

Onlinejobs.ph will create a job posting with the salary listed above.

Virtuallatinos.com or VAs from South America, the base pay will be higher

Facebook Groups (Search "appointment setters and virtual assistants on Facebook, join 10+ groups that have this search title, and post your job posting)

Interview a minimum of five candidates for your VA role. If you just hire the first person you interview, you're likely going to shoot yourself in the foot. You want to make sure that you've had a few conversations with potential candidates because then you will have a feel for which candidate is the right fit. Once you interview your five candidates and you choose the best fit, you need to send that candidate a job offer.

Job Offer Template

Send this information as an email:

Subject Line: Job Offer: Virtual Assistant

Dear (Name),

We are pleased to offer you the position of Virtual Assistant at [Company Name].

This is a full-time position requiring a minimum of eight to ten hours of work a day, five days a week.

Compensation

- Base Salary: $650 USD per week
- Commission: 2% of all new cash sales generated through your efforts.

Your Responsibilities

- Managing my inbox and booking qualified sales calls
- Showing up on time to all training sessions
- Maintaining a high level of performance
- Tracking key metrics related to your job role

Required Skills

- Excellent typing English skills
- Fast paced learner
- Coachable and willing to implement feedback immediately
- Attention to detail

The commission structure is designed to reward your success in generating new business.

Please carefully review this offer. If you accept, please let us know and we'll get you set up with your start date.

I'm excited about the possibility of you joining my team.

Sincerely,
[Your Name]
[Your Company]

When the candidate accepts the job offer, set up an official date to do an onboarding call. On the onboarding call, you're going to go over the expectations of working for you and your company.

These standards should include, but are not limited to:

- Never be late to a shift
- Must provide least one week's notice for all missed shifts, anything less won't be tolerated
- All numbers outlined in the SOPs are expected to be hit every day
- Expectation of a minimum of one booked call a day upon training completion

- Expectation that the VA is always performing at their maximum potential

During the onboarding call, get your VA to sign an onboarding agreement. Here's a template for what that looks like:

You expect that as soon as you hire a VA that they're going to do the job 100% perfect, with no extra training, and be a magic trick who books you sales calls. Unfortunately, that's not how it works, and most online coaches fail at hiring VAs because they don't know how to effectively train them. But don't worry, I'm going to teach you how to properly train your VAs so you don't screw up.

SOPs for VAs

A standard operating procedure, or SOP, means there's a specific way work get's done using a pre-determined set of conditions decided upon by management. Take McDonalds for example. An SOP is why McDonalds' burgers all taste the same no matter what country or continent you get one. That's exactly what you need to create SOPs for your business. You *want*a pre-determined set of conditions your team can follow.

Even if you hire a VA through an agency, you're still responsible for integrating them into your business.

Let's break this into a four-part process:

1. Outline the Expectations
2. Set the Standard

3. Train the Standard
4. Uphold the Standard
5. Raise the Standard

1. Outline the Expectations

To outline the expectations of an SOP, you need to have some documents in order before the VA comes on board. The document you'll need is a Virtual Assistant Workflow. This will give your VA a blueprint to follow regarding how to operate as a VA in your account.

You want to make the step-by-step dummy proof. So, your VA can read the document and be able to clearly understand what their job is, how to effectively do their job, and how to move and function throughout their day.

I've already created the VA workflow for you.

This is only the start of training your VA. In addition, you need to have a library of resources the VA can use for training and support to ensure they effectively know how to do their job. The next thing you need to have in order is ten or more successful screen recordings of how you've successfully booked sales calls with your prospects. These screen recordings need to show the whole process from start to finish.

I also want you to pull together conversations like these:

- Two successful conversations you started with new followers all the way to booked call

- Two successful conversations you started with poll responders on your Instagram Stories.
- Two successful inbound DM conversations that went all the way to booked calls.
- Two successful conversations from application leads all the way through to booked calls.
- Two successful conversations from ads (if you run ads) that show the process all the way through to booked calls.

You're going to screen record these successful conversations by using Loom on your computer, or you can use the screen recording built into your phone. Next, upload your ten examples of successful conversations to a Dropbox or Google Drive folder. Then, I want you to talk through these successful conversations during your screen recording. This gives your VA plenty of evidence to see what successful conversation looks like. This gives them something to compare their work to.

It's important to only do part of scaling your business once you've hit $10,000 or more a month and you know what you're doing. You can't expect your VA to perform when even you don't know how to do your job.

2. Setting the Standard

With your SOPs dialed in, and your videos that show how to do the work, you may expect people are going to just follow along and be able to do exactly what's expected of them. But business isn't like that, and neither is life. People aren't naturally wired to go above and beyond; at our fundamental level we are wired to survive.

For that reason, you need to set the standard of what is acceptable from members of your team and what's not, and you need to set those standards from day one.

It's the same reason you shouldn't hire a VA when you can't book calls for yourself. Whatever standard your business has, your VA is going to adopt that standard when they join the team.

Sure, you can try to fake it, which a lot of people do. You could bring on a VA and tell them, "I want you to book ten calls a week." Yet, you can't even book two calls a week.

Lies always expose themselves, so instead, get to a place where you're booking five to ten sales calls a week by yourself, then bring in a VA to assist you with your lead generation efforts.

The standard is what's acceptable behavior when it comes to your company. The first thing you must do is define what's acceptable. The way you'll do this is by analyzing past data and determining a starting point that is reasonable and acceptable for a new person joining your team. To do this, study your last four weeks of data, including how many calls you booked. Then ask yourself "How many calls, on average, am I booking each week?" If you booked ten last week, two the week before, five the week before, and seven the week before, then you booked twenty-four calls in a month.

That means you booked an average of six calls per week. That becomes your standard.

With a VA, it becomes their job to book your calls. However, it's also your job to continue marketing, which leads to your VA having the opportunity to book calls.

I hear many people say "My VA isn't booking calls." When I look at their social media and see their inconsistent posting schedule or the content they post is subpar, it's easy for me to say, "Sorry, your VA can't draw water from a rock."

Your job is to funnel leads into your inbox by posting high-quality content and consistent value. Your VA's job is to take those conversations and turn them into booked sales calls scheduled on your calendar.

Training the Standard

It's not enough to say "Book six calls a week. Here are the company SOPs. Bye." Why? Because everyone learns a different way. Think about how many times you had to relearn a particular concept before you had a full understanding of it.

You have to train your VA according to your business standards. Make sure that people on your team understand exactly what you want them to do and how you want them to do it. This is why it's impossible to fake it because you can only lead someone where you have already gone yourself.

Here's a formula you can follow to ensure your VA gets up to speed quickly:

1. **Set up the right communication cadence.** For the initial four weeks, meet with your VA every working day for thirty minutes. This guarantees the highest chance of success. Set the meeting for the same time every day. During this time, I want you to train your VA on every individual task on the VA workflow.

2. **Start small then increase activity.** When your VA first joins your team, give them a small task to complete every day. Maybe you have them reply to all comments on your posts and send out a minimum of ten new messages an hour for the first couple of days. Give them a small task. Once they're like, "This is easy boss," gradually increase the load until you are at the full workflow. I believe by the end of week one or two your VA should be at full flow.

3. **Review conversations.** After the initial two weeks, start performing conversation audits. Get on Zoom with your VA and review their conversations from the previous day. Have them bring five names they had full conversations with. I want you to review those conversations and give them feedback. What would you have done differently? Why? Explain your process to your VA and get them to repeat it back to you to show they understand what you mean.

Train your VA like this for the initial four weeks, then you can slowly decrease the meeting frequency to three times a week. As your team grows, you may go back to five to train the new person, then back to three.

I personally have fifteen, full-time VAs who work for me. For six months, I hosted thirty-minute meetings five days a week until they were level ten ninjas.

Now, my VAs work incredibly as a team and they are extremely effective at accomplishing the goal of three-hundred sales calls booked a month through my Instagram.

Holding the Standard

This is the hard part. You must be willing to hold the line when the ball is continuously dropped. I want you to remember this quote forever: "Leaders aren't always liked, but they are respected."

My goal as the leader of a company is not for you to like me. My goal as the leader of a company is to accomplish our goals. Our vision, our ultimate destination, the place that we're headed—it's my responsibility to make sure we get to that place.

For that reason, when my team members aren't performing to the standard that I would like them to be, I make sure that I hold the standard and hold team members accountable and also hold myself accountable. Here's what that looks like:

Let's say the standard on my team is that we book six calls a week. Then we book only two sales calls in a week. First thing I do is look in the mirror. How was I responsible for the decrease in performance? Did I post on social media enough times? Check. Did I post social proof? Check. Did I share CTAs? Check. Have I trained my team properly? Check.

Once I check all my own boxes, *then* I look at my team. If, however, I realize I didn't check a box, then as the leader I hold myself accountable and ensure I check all my boxes. Then, I make a gameplan to solve the problem.

Next, I'm going to meet with my team. I'd handle it by saying:

> Alright guys, last week sucked regarding calls booked, not going to lie. But I'm going to take it on the chin because I didn't do [X] and I believe that's what led to result. So, my gameplan going into

> this week is to do [X] to solve the problem. I need you guys to commit to booking six calls. Cool?"

If, however, I realize that I *did* do my job, and my VA isn't performing, I'd handle it by saying:

> Alright, so last week sucked in terms of calls booked, and I accept full responsibility for this situation. I didn't make the expectations clear for working at this company. The expectations are that we book six sales calls a week and anything less than that number is unacceptable. So, what's going on in the account? What do you guys need my help with so we can make sure that we never dip below six calls again? Anyone have anything they'd like to ask?"

If my VAs don't have any questions, then we'll dig into the conversations until we find the reason we didn't get the results we wanted, and I hold the line. Then, I get them to commit to playing at the new standard, and solving the problem, and I commit myself to doing the training that's necessary to get my team to the standard.

Let's say another week goes by with the same result, and the feedback I gave is not being implemented, so we're still sitting at subpar results with no change. That's when I give a verbal warning during a Zoom meeting.

Here's what I would say:

> We spoke last week about how [X] is the standard and it's still not being met. So, to make sure this never happens again, I am issuing a verbal warning to let you know that this situation cannot happen again because we've already had this conversation. I need you to commit to [X].

The verbal warning should be enough to scare the right person in to line. However, no matter how many times you try to remind some people, they just aren't fully prepared to do what needs to get done to see progress. If that happens, your next step is to issue a written warning. In an email, you'll say. "If [X] happens again, your contract will be terminated."

This is how you must run your team.

Outline the expectations. Set the standard. Train the standard. Uphold the standard.

When you do operate your business like this, you'll have successful team members.

When you consistently hit your targets and goals, then you can raise the standard. Raising the standard means taking your consistent results that you hit back-to-back and begin to set higher targets.

I'm always grateful when my company hits a certain milestone, and I also tell my team that we're the best company in the world in our industry. Being great isn't enough for me; I want to be the best.

Recently, we began hitting six-hundred booked sales calls a month, so I went to my and told them that I wanted to shoot for 750 booked sales call a month. Then, we brainstormed as a team about how we were going to make that number a reality in the next few months.

Scaling Your Business with Boosted Posts

I want to share how to effectively boost a post so you can target people in a specific demographic. I could do an entire book on this topic. I spend $100,000 a month on my Instagram ads. So, I want to give you a formula you can follow and use so you never run out of leads.

Boosting Posts on Instagram

Why do boosted posts work so well? Essentially, you're paying for attention.

I believe that organic marketing is king. Without organic marketing, your ads will be less effective because when someone visits your profile and it's subpar the'll be less likely to follow and engage with you.

However, boosted posts are great, and I'm going to tell you exactly what type of boosted posts to do.

There are three types of boosted posts we need to cover. They are x, x, and x. You can choose the ad type that resonates most and run with it. You can also run all three at the same time and see which one performs best with your audience.

Boosted Post Type One: Previously Published Value Content

When you're consistently posting content that gets views, shares, likes, comments, and grows your follower list, then you can choose your best performing posts on Instagram and boost them. Before you select "boost," understand that the content you're about to spend money on will be seen by complete strangers. So, you want to make sure the content you choose outperformed other content on your page. If it didn't organically do well, then the likelihood of it doing well in front of complete strangers is slim to none.

One thing to note, if you've added copyright-protected music to a post, Instagram likely won't let you boost it or will make you boost your post without sound. To circumvent this, you can repost the video without a copyright-protected song and add it to your video. To find music that isn't protected by copyright, search CapCut or you can screen record non-protected music from TikTok and add it to your videos. If you need help, ask ChatGPT, "How do I add copyright free music as background music on my Instagram Reels?"

I recommend you only boost content that has these three elements:

1. Valuable enough to get results / OR / Storytelling Reel that hits deep
2. Already good engagement organically

3. Aimed at target avatar

If your content doesn't fit these criteria, don't boost it.

Boosted Post Type 2: Follower Ad

A follower ad is exactly what it sounds like. You call out a specific type of person to follow your content and start watching some of the content on your page. Inside of a follower ad, you want to be specific about the type of person you get to follow you from this advertisement, and you want to be clear when doing the "call out" of who they are.

Be very specific with your callout. Then, you want to follow up with some pain points.

> Example: If you are an online personal trainer stuck between $5,000 and $10,000 a month, this is for you.

> Example: You're a great trainer, but you have no idea how to post viral content, get consistent clients, and you're frustrated because your income hasn't grown in months.

Then, add your CTA.

> Example: If this sounds like you, I want you to follow my page and watch my content.

Then, you're going to explain the benefit of following you and watching your content.

> Example: And I'm going to show you exactly how I went from [X] to [X]. Not only that, I've helped this client go from [X] to [X], this client [X] to [X], and this client from [X] to [X].

Next, you'll add one final CTA.

> Example: So, if you're ready to start learning how to get [X] results, then give me a follow and start watching my content.

Boosted Post Type 3: Free Giveaway Ad

This is my favorite type of follower ad in terms of creating conversations for a low dollar amount and providing free value. A free giveaway ad will give you the cheapest leads, but they'll also likely be colder leads because you're using a soft-sell approach. That's based off the theory from hard CTAs versus soft CTAs.

In this type of video, include a specific call out, then give surface level value on the subject. At the end of the video, add a CTA encouraging viewers to follow you and comment with [KEYWORD] to get the resource.

> Example: The reason your online fitness business is stuck below $5,000 a month is because your content plan sucks.

Here's the callout example: But don't worry, I know how to help. Here is a content schedule that's designed to get you five clients every week.

Tell them why they should pay attention.

Example:

> On Monday, you're going to post a hard CTA. People fall off track on the weekends and you want to catch them when they're motivated to work toward their goal again.
>
> Then on Thursday, you're going to post a soft CTA. With this post, you're going to provide a free

giveaway in exchange for a comment and this will generate new conversations.

And if you want the full schedule that includes exactly what to post on your Newsfeed and your Instagram Stories on the other days, make sure you're following me and comment the word PLAN. Then, I'll send over the full schedule.

Make sure your free resource is beneficial because if someone leaves a comment and the free resource isn't helpful, they won't come back to your content again.

How to Boost Posts

Apple just started charging a service fee, which means it's more expensive to boost Instagram posts from your phone. So, visit the Instagram homepage using your computer to boost your posts.

Here's the step-by-step instructions to boost your Instagram posts:

13. Choose the post you want to boost.
14. Select "Boost Reel" on the post itself.
15. Choose the "Visit your profile" option.

    Tap "Create your own audience." Don't let Instagram choose your audience; the ad won't perform well.

16. Turn off Advantage+ audience, it's not good.
17. Label your audience, so you know which audience this is for future uses.
18. Choose Location. I use Canada and U.S., but choose the country you live in.

19. Choose your interests. Keep your selections broad but specific.
    a. If you're an online fitness coach, I recommend: Fitness, Health, and Business.
    b. If you're a relationship coach, I recommend: Relationships and Family.
    c. If you're a mindset coach, I recommend: Mindset, Business, and Fitness.
20. Keep the targeting broad within a specific subject matter because Facebook and Instagram will automatically optimize it to the right audience if you let the algorithm do its job.
21. Choose your age demographics. I never go lower than twenty-two years old, but it will depend on your industry.
22. Choose gender if it's relevant to your niche.
23. Save your selections.
24. Set your budget anywhere between $10 to $20 dollars a day.
25. Choose "Run this ad until I pause it."
26. Boost your post.

THEREALBRIANMARK
Posts
10K PER MONTH BUSINESS TOOLS
DM Automation
16.7K · View insights
Boost post
253
12
159
Liked by geisha_fitness and others

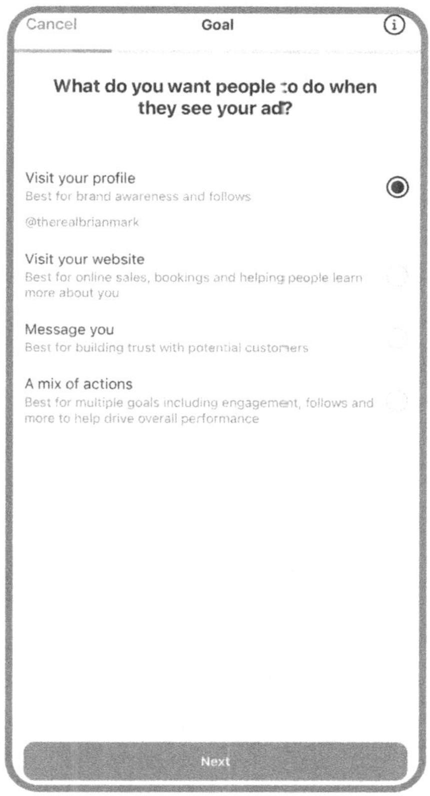
Cancel
Goal
What do you want people to do when they see your ad?
Visit your profile
Best for brand awareness and follows
@therealbrianmark
Visit your website
Best for online sales, bookings and helping people learn more about you
Message you
Best for building trust with potential customers
A mix of actions
Best for multiple goals including engagement, follows and more to help drive overall performance
Next

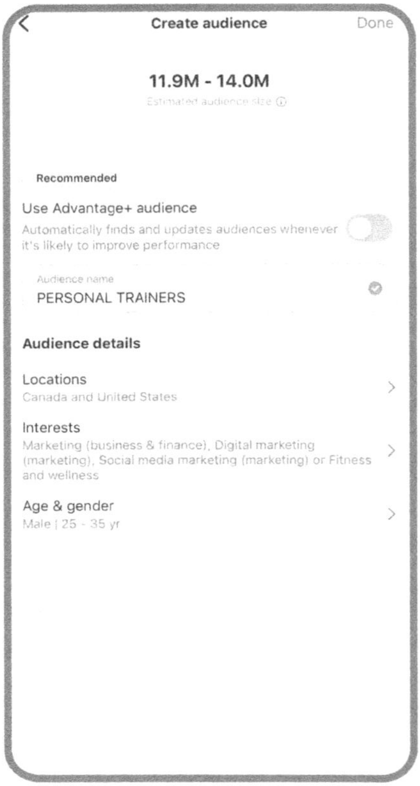

How to Analyze Boosted Post Performance

For your boosted Reels, you want to get your cost per follower into the $2 to $7 range at the max end.

Some of my clients pay 50 cents per follower, which is awesome! This typically happens on a video that starts out with how they used to look (3 second video) then shows them now (3 second video). Their caption says, "Follow to learn how."

One dollar per follower is very good. Two dollars per follower is good. Four dollars per follower is still good as long as it's quality leads. Seven to eight dollars is the highest I want to pay per new follower and the *only* reason I'd want the price per followr this high is if I specifically spoke to my target audience and said, "If you are an online fitness coach who is stuck under

$5,000 a month." There's only going to be a certain number of people who fall into that category, so naturally Meta will have to show my Reel to more people in order for me to gain followers. That's why that number cost per new follower rate is higher.

Once you find a Reel that consistently brings you followers and you're able to start new conversations with them as soon as they join your page, you'll never run out of leads.

That's how you solve a lead flow issue.

SUMMARY

In this chapter, I taught you how to hire, train, and integrate VAs into your business. Next, I taught you how to create a job posting, as well as how to interview, hire, and onboard a VA. Then you learned what an SOP is and how to create them, in addition to how to effectively train your VAs.

Next, I gave you a blueprint for setting the standard, raising the standard, and upholding the standard within your team. We ended this chapter with how to run boosted posts so you never have a lead flow problem.

CHAPTER 12

CONCLUSION

You live in the greatest day in age that's ever happened in the history of mankind when it comes to building a business. Not only do you have instant access to a super computer through your phone, you also have access to a library of encyclopedias with ChatGPT.

There has never been a better time to be a human being who wants to build their own business and dream life. The ability to transition between income classes during your lifetime, has never been easier. Imagine trying to move up from a peasant to a president two hundred years ago. You'd end up dead for even considering it.

And yet here we are. We had a boy from a small town in Austria who not only became a bodybuilding champion, but also a movie star, and then the governor of California. He did so with public favor and opinion. Now we have a businessman who ran for president and was elected because of the power of social media.

Can you see what's happening right in front of your eyes? Why have you not made the decision to take part in this revolution?

More than likely, you had no idea how to do it. But now you do. You have the entire blueprint.

Information without implementation, however, is just noise. Don't be the person who reads this book and then never does anything with the information.

I urge you, I implore you, I best you, take this seriously. The foundations I gave you in this book are the exact same foundations I've used to scale my online coaching business to more than thirty million dollars in sales.

They are also the exact same foundations I've used to create twenty millionaires. Now, you have access to the same foundational principles that have built more than ten thousand successful online fitness businesses. It's your time.

The only way you're going to get anywhere in this life is making the decision that it's you. You're the one who changes your story. You're the one who rewrites your family's name. You're the one who breaks the generational curse. You're the one who's going to be the leader your family and friends need.

This business takes absolutely zero money to start and provides returns bigger than any investment you can make, including cryptocurrency, stocks, bonds, and real estate.

You might be reading this with two hundred followers and no social media experience. So was my client, Clayton Snyder. He started a new Instagram account four years ago and now is generating more than seventy thousand dollars in cash collected revenue every month.

I also understand if you have a massive following but haven't made any money from it yet. That was my client, Christian. He had five-hundred thousand followers and was still working as a valet making two thousand dollars a month because he didn't know how to sell. His first month working with me he generated forty thousand dollars.

It's not that hard. I've made it simple for you to understand. This industry is not going anywhere. For all the people who say, "the online coaching industry is saturated," that's like saying "the business world is saturated." There are lot of businesses on the market; there are also a lot of businesses on the market that suck.

Just like there's a lot of online coaches on the market and there's also a lot of online coaches who have no idea how to effectively promote themselves, how to write content, how to properly DM, how to book sales calls, and how to make money.

Now you do! Go make some money.

Take charge of your goals—apply now
and let's build your success story together!

LET'S CONNECT

Find me @therealbrianmark on Instagram, The Change Lives Make Money Online Trainer Podcast, and Brian Mark on YouTube.

YOUTUBE

INSTAGRAM

PODCAST

www.ingramcontent.com/pod-product-compliance
Lightning Source LLC
LaVergne TN
LVHW022204200926
848481LV00006B/1841